D0044251

Alice + Freda Forever

From A. to F.

Alice + Freda Forever

A MURDER IN MEMPHIS

ALEXIS COE

With illustrations by
SALLY KLANN

AN IMPRINT OF
ZEST BOOKS

35 Stillman Street, Suite 121
San Francisco, CA 94107
www.zestbooks.net

CONNECT WITH ZEST!

zestbooks.net/blog
zestbooks.net/contests
twitter.com/zestbooks
facebook.com/zestbook
facebook.com/BooksWithATwist
pinterest.com/zestbooks

History / True Crime / Gender Studies
Library of Congress data available
ISBN: 978-1-936976-60-7

Jacket design by Adam Grano
Interior design by Adam Grano and Dagmar Trojanek

Manufactured in the U.S.A.
DOC 10 9 8 7 6 5 4 3 2 1
4500485180

FOR

ALICE MITCHELL
(1872–1898)

AND

FREDA WARD
(1874–1892)

TABLE OF CONTENTS

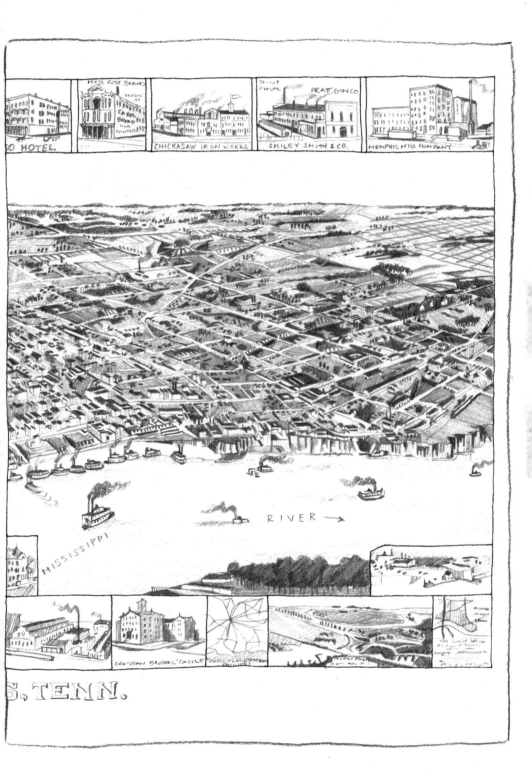

O HOTEL.

MOSS ROSE BRAND

CHICKASAW IRON WORKS

PRATT GIN CO

SMILEY SMITH & CO.

MEMPHIS MILL COMPANY

RIVER →

MISSISSIPPI

CHRISTIAN BROTHERS' COLLEGE

S, TENN.

MAIN CHARACTERS

ALICE MITCHELL

NICKNAMES: *Allie, Alvin J. Ward,*
AJW, Freda Myra Ward

FREDERICA WARD

NICKNAMES: *Freda, Fred, Freddie,*
Patty Sing, Pitty Sing, Sing, Serg. Jueq

ALICE MITCHELL'S FAMILY

George Mitchell, *father*
Isabella Mitchell, *mother*
Robert Mitchell, *older brother*
Frank Mitchell, *older brother*
Mattie Mitchell, *eldest sister*
Addie Mitchell, *older sister*

FREDA WARD'S FAMILY

Thomas Ward, *father*
Ada Volkmar, *eldest sister/surrogate mother*
Jo Ward, *older sister*, NICKNAME: *Joe*
William Volkmar, *brother-in-law/Ada's husband*

JUDGE, DEFENSE, AND PROSECUTION

Julius DuBose, *Judge*
Colonel George Gantt, *defense*
General Luke Wright, *defense*
Malcolm Rice Patterson, *defense*
George Peters, *prosecution*

MISCELLANEOUS

Lillie Johnson, *Alice's best friend*, NICKNAME: *Jessie Rita James*
Ashley Roselle, *suitor/romantic rival*
Lucy Franklin, *Mitchell family cook*

INTRODUCTION

WHEN I FIRST LEARNED about the 1892 murder of seventeen-year-old Freda Ward by her ex-fiancé, nineteen-year-old Alice Mitchell, I was riding a New York City subway on my long commute home from graduate school. I remember it well because I was so engrossed in the act of imagining their lives, I missed my stop—and then three more. I'd been reading a scholarly article about the case, but I kept losing Alice and Freda in the academic talk of identity politics and American modernity.[1] And so I'd closed my eyes and tried to hear their voices through the dense text, to visualize their story.

But I had little more than a train ride for such reveries. I was already a year into research on citizenship, and I was determined to be the kind of historian who focused on law, not love. Nevertheless, I slowly started collecting newspaper articles about the Mitchell-Ward case, struck by their sensational headlines and front page placement, and intrigued by the physical evidence they mentioned—love letters, a bottle of poison, a father's razor.

After I graduated, I worked as a research curator in the Exhibitions Department at the New York Public Library. With my personal collection of Alice and Freda materials growing, and my experience in public engagement deepening, I began to picture different ways of sharing their story. I longed to tell it on the page—as a nonfiction narrative, not a study—accompanied by the kind of stirring visuals an exhibition case offered.

I imagined a book that was both written and curated. I wanted readers to *see* my research, to explore the archival mix, connect with the material, and draw their own conclusions.

Six years after I missed my subway stop, I found myself walking through Elmwood Cemetery, led by Vincent Astor, a local historian in Memphis, Tennessee. I was, at this point, thoroughly consumed by the sad tale of Alice and Freda. The closer we got to their graves, the heavier my body felt. I reminded myself, as I always do when approaching that very last folder in an archive: *you already know how the story ends.* But the truth is, you never really know.

Just then, as I was gingerly sidestepping graves, Vincent paused for a moment and turned to me. "If you're remembering their names and telling their stories," he said in a gliding, Southern drawl, "they won't mind if you're stepping on their toes."

In this book, I hope to have done just that. Alice and Freda's names—once well known across America—are now recognized by only a small group of people, and yet, their tragic story will feel familiar. They were teenagers in love, and they planned to spend the rest of their lives together. Their relationship—plagued by issues of jealousy and infidelity from the very beginning—was fraught, in no small part, because it was illicit. In 1892 Memphis, few people had heard of same-sex love, and even fewer believed it was anything less than perverse.

And from the moment the romantic nature of Alice and Freda's relationship was discovered, that was all they heard: It was wrong. It was unnatural. It was impossible. It was forbidden.

There is a good deal of fault to be found in both Alice and Freda—most clearly, of course, in Alice's unconscionable act of violence—but two women loving each other, and wanting to make a home and a life together, is not one of them. And yet, when Freda was six feet underground and Alice behind bars, it was Alice's motivation—love, and not the bloody murder—that was said to be insane. Alice was driven mad by a perverse passion, medical experts would testify. Their observations were recycled time and time again; more than 120 years later, today's readers will find much of that world is sadly familiar to us.

While I offer historical context in the pages that follow, this is very much about Alice and Freda's short-lived romance. To tell that story—with so few primary sources, and even fewer trustworthy ones among them— I have strained to hear their voices in the archives, newspapers, medical journals, school catalogs, courtroom proceedings, and of course, their love letters. When there was agreement among sources, I made note of it, and gave those quotations priority. From the very beginning, I noticed obvious fabrications driven by various agendas, and I wrote that in, too. In order to bring the reader closer to historical actors, to hear their voices, I pulled dialogue from courtroom testimony and newspaper articles. In this same vein, the book presents the reader with over a hundred visual elements.

Artist Sally Klann illustrated many of the documents and artifacts I found in the archives in Memphis, and also outside of it; the design motif in the chapter headings was inspired by the gates seen throughout Memphis, and in particular, the entrance to Elmwood Cemetery, where Alice, Freda, and many other people who appear in this book are buried. Sally artistically interpreted the domestic scenes and courtroom proceedings I describe in the text, illuminating intimate moments and, in darkly funny turns, imagining how the faulty reasoning of some of our historical actors leads to absurd conclusions.

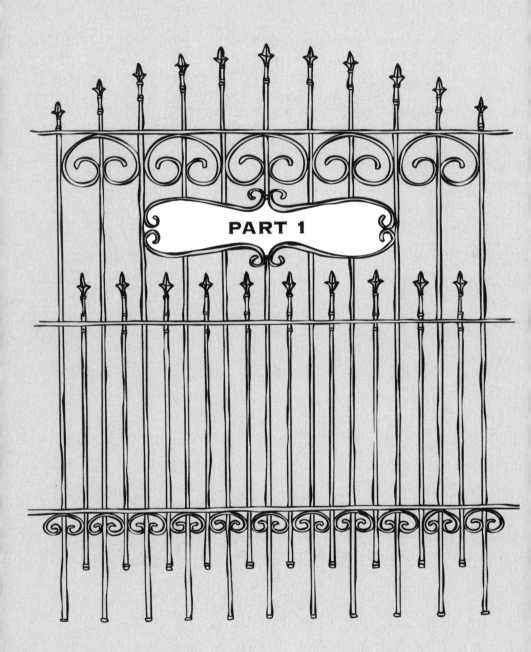

PART 1

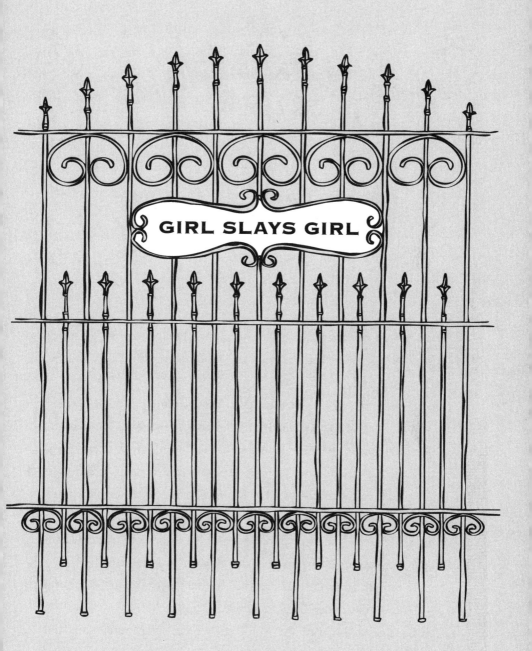

GIRL SLAYS GIRL

CHAPTER ONE

I DON'T CARE IF I'M HUNG!

FOR DAYS ON END, heavy snow descended on Memphis. The roads were slick with ice and the wind was chilling, but for Alice Mitchell, home was no refuge. It had become her prison.

Every morning, nineteen-year-old Alice arose from yet another sleepless night to find a landscape unaltered, a city blanketed in white. Through the frosted windowpane, she watched her father and brothers come and go as they pleased. No one questioned their trips downtown or suggested their business could wait until the weather improved. But the Mitchell women were governed by a different set of rules. And what would Alice say on her own behalf? The truth was not an option, and she could conjure no lie convincing enough to justify exposing herself to the tempest outside.

So she waited, enduring one anxious, blustery day after another, until finally, darkness descended, and the house fell quiet.

If it continued this way, she would miss Freda Ward altogether. But Alice refused to let that happen. She had made a solemn declaration, and she intended to make good on it.

In the meantime, she could find no solace in her house, no distraction through sewing or reading. Alice had no interest in food, in eating it or making it, and yet she spent most of her waking hours in the kitchen, where she had hidden the locked box. She would spend hours studying its treasures: the love letters, the photograph, the engagement ring. It was an archive of heartbreak. It was all she had left.

Alice had shown the ring to Lucy Franklin, the Mitchell family's African American cook, and shared her tale of star-crossed love, how her hopes for the future had been so cruelly dashed by disapproving relations. Even though Lucy was a captive audience, she felt genuine concern for young Alice, and tried as best she could to console her. This went on for months, but Alice withheld parts of the story from Lucy, allowing assumptions to stand in the place of truth. Over time, Alice's inconsistent narrative grew confusing, but as Lucy would later testify, it hardly mattered. As far as she was concerned, the story became secondary to Alice's manner, unsettling to the point of distraction.

But there was no one Alice could truly confide in. Certainly not her mother, who had forbidden her to see Freda, nor her older sisters, who had long ago dismissed her as anxious. Even Lillie Johnson, her closest friend, was ignorant of the truth, and she had been there from the very beginning.

Only Freda knew the whole story, and she wanted nothing to do with Alice anymore. It was as if their love had never existed, her world shattered by a phantom. The box, hidden in the kitchen, was all she had left, the only proof that Freda had ever loved her.

Before the snow had come, Alice would often claim the family's buggy and invite Lillie to ride downtown, a social call that conveniently masked her true goal of surveillance. But the weather that week had often made prisoners of them all.

Twenty-five days into the New Year, 1892, Alice awoke to a clear sky on the very day she needed it. It was nearly three o'clock by the time she carefully steered the newly shod horses along the thawing roads to Lillie's house. Her friend was caring for a young nephew, but nonetheless readily accepted the invitation, wrapping herself and the boy in jackets and hats, gloves and scarves. They soon settled into the buggy alongside Alice, completely unaware of her plan. The only warning sign was carefully hidden away in her dress pocket.

THERE WAS NOTHING UNUSUAL about two young women from respectable families spending a Monday afternoon aimlessly riding through downtown Memphis. No one expected them to spend this fleeting time between school and marriage attending college or working. There was little for them to do but check the post office, call on male relations at work, and perhaps treat their young charge to a sugary treat. But it was Alice who held the reins that day, and she had been steering the buggy toward Hernando Street all along.

Lillie was generally obtuse when it came to Alice, to a degree a grand jury would soon find suspect. She had played accomplice on enough of Alice's investigative missions that month to know why her friend slowed the horses to a near-halt before the widow Kimbrough's home. Freda and her older sister, Jo Ward, had been staying there for nearly a month, during which time they had shown no interest in Alice and Lillie, once their closest friends at the Higbee School for Young Ladies.

Lillie had adjusted to this reality, but Alice could not. The Ward sisters had moved up the river to Golddust, but visited Memphis often. In the old days, they had almost always stayed with Alice. In the weeks leading up to such happy reunions, she and Freda would exchange a flurry of letters, with much consideration given to sleeping arrangements. The goal was always to spend the night together, alone in Alice's bed.

But when Alice learned the Ward sisters were in town these days, it was by vigilance or luck. Her sleuthing had yielded general information about this visit—they would be coming sometime after Christmas, likely staying with Mrs. Kimbrough—but nothing more. And so, Alice went on self-imposed surveillance duty, riding and walking on Hernando Street as often as she could, hoping to see Freda through the window, or better yet, to run into her on the street.

Alice had been trying to contact Freda for months. Her letters were returned unopened, or presumably discarded, until finally, just a week earlier, Alice received a response, though it offered her no comfort. Freda admitted to being in Memphis, but momentarily leaving on the *Rosa Lee*—an impossibility. The city had practically come to a wintry standstill, and everyone knew the steamers were running on an irregular schedule. Alice studied every line of the letter, each crammed full of lies and broken promises, and grew apoplectic over her ex-fiancé's sloppy attempt to deceive her. The *Rosa Lee* had most certainly not gone out, and neither had the Ward sisters.

On January 25, however, the *Ora Lee* was due to depart. If they had not left already, Alice seemed certain they would leave before sundown on this steamer. If she were right, Freda and Jo would have to leave Mrs. Kimbrough's house soon. This was her moment.

Through equal parts perseverance and chance, Alice had learned how to unravel Freda's lies over the years, and sure enough, from atop the inching buggy, she watched as the front door of the widow Kimbrough's home swung open—and her dear Freda emerged. She was followed by Jo and another friend, Christina Purnell. They moved toward bustling Front Street, just north of the customhouse, blithely unaware of the buggy slowly pursuing them along the busy streets of downtown Memphis. They pushed past the businessmen and workers heading in all different directions, gingerly sidestepping women clutching their skirts, all the while tiptoeing carefully over patches of ice and mud.

This time, Alice had been right. It was clear they were headed toward the waterfront. If Freda boarded the *Ora Lee* for Golddust, there would be no guarantee she would return to Memphis any time soon, if at all. She might just marry one of the young men she corresponded with, and move even farther away. Alice knew this might be her last chance.

And what did Freda know, as she made her way to the docks? She knew there was only one way out of their engagement, just as she knew Alice was not one to break promises.[2]

THE SURE-FOOTED HORSES PROVED FAR STEADIER on the slippery, thawing ground than Freda, Jo, and Christina had. Distracted by frequent stops to steady themselves, they did not seem to notice when Alice's buggy passed them. Their slow advance offered plenty of time for Alice to settle the horses in front of the post office, climb down, and watch the trio approach. Alice's eyes locked on Freda.

She searched Freda's face for an invitation, open to a wide range of signals. In days long gone, Freda had gone on about the many expressions she pulled, each look imbued with meaning. And now, despite all evidence to the contrary, Alice was sure, at the moment the young women passed by, that she had seen Freda wink with her right eye. It meant, "I love you."

It was the sign Alice had been waiting for all along, and she took it as an invitation. The time had come.

"Where are you going?" Lillie called out from the buggy, as Alice sprinted off in Freda's direction.[3]

"I am going to see Fred once more," she shouted over her shoulder, using her pet name for Freda. Lillie stayed behind. The horses needed looking after, and so did her nephew, but in truth, Alice had never invited her to come along. It was not going to be that kind of parting.

Freda was not faring well on the slippery slope. She stopped often to regain her balance, while Alice moved toward her with determination. By the time they reached the north gate of the customhouse grounds, Alice was upon them.

Alice reached into her dress pocket, her fingers sliding over Freda's last letter, in search of her father's razor. She had been carrying it around for months, waiting and plotting, but the grade leading down to the water-front was not the destination she had imagined. Alice knew where people congregated, and where the crowd thinned. She needed to get Freda alone. There could be no intervention.

The streets swirled with faces, both familiar and not, allowing Alice to move undetected. She had hoped it would remain this way until they reached the steamer, but Christina Purnell noticed their old friend suddenly lurking beside them. There was no more time to waste. Turning from Christina's disbelieving eyes, Alice leaned in toward Freda's face, as if to kiss her cheek.

"Oh!" Freda shrieked.

"You dirty dog!" Jo screamed as she watched blood pour down her sister's neck, staining her dress red. She grasped the only weapon she had, the long umbrella in her hand, and lunged toward Alice.

It was no match for the razor. Alice had only intended to harm one Ward sister that day, but the umbrella enraged her, and she turned her blood soaked razor on Jo, slicing at her collarbone.

"Leave my sister alone!" Jo yelled, with now her own gaping wound. She had lost her only means of defense. In the scuffle, Alice had gotten hold of the umbrella, and proved more successful in using it. She lunged at Freda, knocking off her hat.

"Alice, you dirty dog," Jo screamed again, a last ditch effort to distract her as Freda made a dash for the boat. "You'll hang for this!"

"I don't care if I'm hung! I want to die anyhow," Alice shouted back.

A pool of blood stood in Freda's place, and Alice, seeing that it formed a trail toward the steamer, took off in its direction. Bleeding and disoriented, Freda struggled even more on the icy slope, allowing Alice to easily catch up.

It took just one more slice, this one all the way across her throat, before Freda crumpled onto the ground.

And that was when Alice noticed people moving toward them, their eyes focused on Freda. Alice had only realized half of her plan—but the rest would have to wait. Razor in hand, she sprinted back up the hill, leaving the love of her life bleeding on the railroad tracks.

THE GREAT DRAMA

ALICE AND FREDA MET at the Higbee School for Young Ladies, where well-to-do white Memphians sent their daughters. Together, they roamed the hallways with Freda's older sister, Jo, and Alice's best-friend, Lillie. The foursome was well known, as was their coupling. Alice and Freda had made no attempt to hide their relationship: their kissing and hugging and hand-holding was certainly noted by those around them. But Jo and Lillie were also seen with their arms linked, sharing meaningful glances and speaking in hushed voices.

During the Victorian era, proper American women were not to speak of their desire for men, let alone show it, but demonstrative relationships with other women were considered unremarkable. In Memphis, "chumming" was the regional term for intimate female friendships, but it was by no means particular to Eastern Tennessee. The poet Henry Wadsworth Longfellow called these romantic friendships a "rehearsal in girlhood of the great drama of woman's life," a kind of training ground for the main event, the courtship by a young woman's future husband.[4]

But for Alice, this was no rehearsal.

In Europe, sexologists were just beginning to define same-sex love, but this nascent research had barely reached American soil; the word lesbian would not be in circulation for another forty years. In the South, a white woman from a respectable family was bombarded with a consistent message at home, school, and church: She was expected to play the role of wife, and then the role of mother to as many children as her husband desired. A couple like Alice and Freda had no name for what they felt for each other, no adults to advise or serve as examples, and certainly no literature to call upon.

They went to the theater often enough to know that actresses could play male roles convincingly, but that was likely the furthest either of them saw gender boundaries pushed—and even then, this deviance was safely contained within the realm of playacting, much like the notion of chumming itself. Once the curtain came crashing down and the house lights blinded the audience, the rules of society were reinstated. The actresses discarded men's costumes in favor of their own dresses, as if to acknowledge their male characters belonged within a very small and specific space, for a limited time only.

American newspapers would later speculate that French fiction, full of risqué tales of same-sex love and other noteworthy acts by libertines, had possibly influenced Freda's murder. But even if English translations of books by novelists Honoré de Balzac, George Sand, or Théophile Gautier made it to Memphis, it was unlikely that Alice would have happened upon them.

If Alice had indeed read those French novels, she might have realized that other women shared her desires. She seemed to feel trapped by emotions she understood to be unique, and may have taken some comfort in the idea that there were other women in the world to love and, more importantly, who would love her back.

But would French novels have really made a difference, either way? Alice's obsession with Freda was so great, so all encompassing, that any tale of alternate domesticity was unlikely to alter their tragic ending—even if the tale was their own.[5]

FREDA WAS FAR MORE CAPRICIOUS with her affections, as Alice would soon realize, but in 1891, their greatest challenge was geographical. Freda's eldest sister, Mrs. Ada Volkmar, had moved to Golddust, a small town on the Mississippi River, and their father, the widower Thomas Ward, soon followed. He relied on Ada to look after Freda and Jo, but the new city offered him more than just help with his younger daughters. Back in Memphis, Thomas had been a machinist at a fertilizer company, but in Golddust, he was able to work as a merchant and a planter. Things were looking up for the Ward family.

Alice and Freda had no choice but to make the best of it. They no longer lived in the same city, but when they visited each other, they did so for weeks at a time. Every day was spent together, every moment precious.

The nights were advantageous, too. After they kissed their families goodnight, it was expected that they would share a bed, their bodies close, their movements obscured under the covers.

Long visits spent in such close proximity had a downside, too. It became harder for Freda to hide her infidelities from Alice, and even harder still to escape her anger over them.

Late one night in December, the Mitchell home was still. The entire family, with the exception of Alice, was fast asleep. She lay in bed, alongside Freda, wide awake. In her hand, she clutched a bottle marked POISON.

Before falling asleep, Freda had admitted to loving not one, but two men. The sun would rise soon enough, ushering in the day Freda would return to Golddust, where she would once again move freely, far from Alice's watchful gaze. As the hours passed, Alice concluded that either she or Freda would have to die. Laudanum, a potent mix of opium and alcohol, was easy to procure for various aches and pains, but it came with a warning. The solution was highly concentrated, and fatal overdoses were not uncommon. If Alice could get enough past Freda's lips while her beloved slept, the drink would likely be her last.

Alice would eventually write out a more comprehensive list—"How to Kill"—but that night laudanum was her only option, and she could hardly guarantee there was enough for both of them. And so she lay there, inches from her love, contemplating how many doses she held in her hand.

And that was the scene that greeted Freda when her eyes fluttered open. She was sharing a bed with a young woman who was deciding whether or not to kill her. The night was fraught, with Alice openly brandishing the bottle, and Freda too scared to close her eyes—and yet, Freda stayed in that bed with Alice. She never called for help, and she never told the Mitchells, or her own family, what had happened.

Daybreak did nothing to quell the drama. Laudanum in hand, Alice followed Freda onboard the steamer that would soon leave for Golddust, cornered her in the stateroom, and locked the door behind them.

"Marry whomever you want," she said, and downed the bottle herself.

DIE, ALICE DID NOT, but the aftermath could not have been pretty. A laudanum overdose did not guarantee death, but symptoms like insufferably itchy skin, constricted breathing, and obstructed bowels may have made her wish it had.

If nothing else, it was clear that Alice needed a better plan, one that took control of the situation. If things continued this way, Freda would be married soon enough. She might settle in Golddust, near her family, or

THE
HIGBEE SCHOOL
FOR
YOUNG + LADIES

HIGBEE SCHOOL
BEALE, LAUDERDALE
AND
JESSAMINE ST
MEMPHIS,
TENN

worse yet, move to where her husband's people lived. Alice needed to find a way to possess her love completely, to make her ineligible to all bachelors.

Alice's own future would soon come into question as well. Whether she liked it or not, the cult of domesticity was the prevailing value system in the United States and Britain, and it identified the home as the proper sphere for women of Alice's race and class. She had certainly been told this at Miss Higbee's. The first page of the school's catalog stated its educational aim quite clearly: "The Systematic Development of True Womanhood."[6] The four cardinal virtues—piety, purity, submissiveness, and domesticity—were not only taught in schools, but reinforced by magazines, cookbooks, newspapers, literature, and in church every Sunday.[7]

Alice was adept at discouraging suitors, but that would be difficult to maintain, especially if her family forced the issue. If she relented to pressure and married, there would be babies, one after the other, both her own or those of her siblings. She would be expected to help maintain the household, with little-to-no autonomy or authority over anything, including her own body.

If she did not marry, her father and brothers would decide her fate. The options in that scenario were clear: Alice could continue to live in her parents' home, as her older sisters had, or with her married siblings.

Alice seemed to want out of the Mitchell home and into her own, but it was not as if she could just go out and get an apartment, or the job she would need to pay for it. Occupations for women were extremely limited in the 1890s, especially for her class. Of the 8,200 women employed in Memphis in 1891, 2,200 were white, and the majority of these wage earners were servants and seamstresses, and they still ended up in someone else's home, whether it was their family's, their employer's, or a boarding house. They were rarely from well-to-do families like the Mitchells, working out of necessity, and yet, only about three percent made enough to claim economic independence.[8]

One way or another, a man would be the head of Alice's home, and she would live the kind of life he saw fit. The other Mitchell women seemed perfectly happy to spend day after day inside, with women like Lucy Franklin tending to the household's daily demands. Their hours were spent in a state of perpetual anticipation, filled with leisurely activities like mending and knitting, writing letters, and reading the Bible. Whether they enjoyed these tasks, or regarded them as mere distractions was immaterial; everything depended on the Mitchell men. Any time Alice's father and brothers came in the front door, their needs were prioritized above all else.

The kind of power Alice craved, the right to come and go as she pleased and, most importantly, fully dominate Freda, could only be wielded by a man.

And so Alice would have to figure out a way to become one.

CHAPTER THREE

MR. AND MRS. ALVIN J. WARD

ALICE HAD YET TO FIGURE OUT how to transform herself—a plump, handsome woman—into a man, but she knew how to act like one. If a man wanted to spend the rest of his life with a woman, he proposed, and in February of 1891, Alice did just that. She could not make her intentions known to Freda's family or procure Thomas Ward's permission, but she could ask Freda to marry her, and that was all that mattered. She sent the proposal in a letter, and in return, she received a fervid acceptance.

Still, Alice sent two more letters, each one containing the same proposal. Acceptance was binding, she warned, and Freda agreed to her terms each time, posting an equal number of sanguine letters back to Memphis.

Of course, it would be nearly thirty years before women had the right to vote in America, and more than 120 years after Alice and Freda's engagement, same-sex marriage is still illegal in the state of Tennessee.

But for Alice and Freda, these were just details, minor problems in need of creative solutions.

————

They devoted themselves to the task with absolute secrecy. Alice's brother, Robert Mitchell, would later recount their letters in court, many of which emphasized Freda's role as a "true woman," an obedient, faithful wife.

In another document, Alice gives her ideas of what a model wife ought to be and do. She must never deceive, must know how to keep house, must know how to cook, she must be able to sew on a button and must be her first love and her last love. She closes the essay by saying if a certain brown-eyed girl keeps her promise she will show a model husband and wife within a year. This reference is, of course, to Freda.[9]

At the time, however, no one, not even Jo or Lillie, suspected anything out of the ordinary existed between them, and Alice was determined to keep it that way—even if it meant denying herself in the present.

May 12

I started this last night, but will finish it now. I don't think I will stay all night with you Friday. I suppose you know why. You were two weeks after me before, and it will be two weeks Friday since you stayed all night with me. As it is Joe's time to stay with me, I don't think I will get to sleep with you.

Sing, I have a rose for you; if it is not withered by the next time I see you, I will give it to you. I have been trying to get one for a long time. It beats all other roses. Good-bye.

ALLIE

A nineteenth-century reader would not have suspected the dispatch was actually a love letter, even though it was teeming with machinations.[10] Every turn of phrase could be explained through the lens of a tender, albeit impassioned, female friendship. There was nothing unusual in the politics of cliques reaching a fevered pitch during sleepovers, especially over sleeping arrangements. Alice appears considerate in her letter; she wants Freda to know that she prefers her, but does not wish to injure the feelings of another.

Exchanging small gifts was equally unremarkable. If the rose Alice mentions was not a euphemism, it was a perfectly respectable gift. It not only suggested affection for gardens, an acceptable interest for proper young women, but it was also very thoughtful. There was some effort involved in procuring the perfect rose, and perhaps it was of particular importance to Freda, who no longer lived in Memphis, but may have shown an attachment to its flora.

The rose was hardly the most lavish gift Alice bestowed on her intended. She had been secretly saving small sums of money, the bulk of which she reserved for their elopement and setting up house, but in June, she made one large purchase: an engagement ring for Freda. She obviously gave the purchase much thought and consideration, engraving the ring, "From A. to F." And of course, she told no one about it.

Freda was far less discreet, happy to display their love whenever possible—the more conspicuous and dramatic, the better. To avoid suspicion, Alice argued that they should be no more demonstrative than Jo and Lillie. She thought further exhibitionism put their future in peril.

But to Alice, it was worse than imprudent—the lack of seriousness this immodest behavior implied seemed to really bother her. Schoolgirls went chumming as an imitation of what was to come, not living what had already arrived. Couples who were betrothed in earnest, which is what Alice believed them to be, did not behave that way.

Either way, in order to make it to the altar without suspicion, Alice reasoned they should appear to be the unexceptional half of a socially acceptable quartet.

IF ALICE HAD A POST-ENGAGEMENT POLICY, it was to pass. They were to continue to pass as girls chumming, and then later, Alice was to pass as man. At first, it was a practical measure, a necessary façade until a long-term plan could be formed, but over time, it became the plan itself. Passing as a man was more than just a way to hide a relationship between two women; as a man, she could claim all of the rights and responsibilities of a husband, too.

Alice never expressed a desire to be a man for any other reason than marrying Freda, so there is little to suggest that she saw impersonation as anything more than a means to that end. She may have been inspired by examples from history. Joan of Arc kept her hair short and wore military attire while fighting the English during the Hundred Years' War, and in America, hundreds of women passed as soldiers in the Union and Confederate armies during the Civil War.

Alice had definitely seen actresses disguised in men's clothing, wigs, and makeup at the theater, and it seemed to influence her transformation—the adornments, that is, but not the gestures. If she studied the mannerisms and word choices of men, practiced deepening her voice and displaying the chivalrous behavior expected from Southern gentlemen, she made no mention of it. She did, however, discuss ordering a suit and fashioning her hair into a style worn by young men. If it would please Freda, Alice promised to grow a mustache. She would shave the loosely scattered, light hairs that grew above her upper lip, hoping that each new growth would get her closer to darker, bristly stubble.

Freda, who longed to be on the stage, was delighted that their plan now contained wardrobe considerations. She played an active role in shaping Alice's character, mixing elements from their old life with that of their new one, as husband and wife. Freda loved calling Alice by her pet name, Allie, and thought "Alvin J. Ward" to be a similar, agreeable name.

It was careless to keep Freda's last name, an obvious clue for whomever the family would inevitably send after them, but it was just one of several curious choices the couple made. Even though Mr. and Mrs. Alvin J. Ward wisely opted not to settle in Memphis, a city teeming with people who knew them and their families, they nevertheless planned to marry there.

Even stranger still, Freda promised to enlist her own family's reverend from Grace Episcopal Church to perform the marriage ceremony. Freda was said to have had a lovely singing voice, and when the Wards lived in Memphis, she often performed at the church. It is hard to imagine that the reverend, who had so often seen the seventeen-year-old surrounded by the Wards, would officiate Freda's nuptials without questioning her family's conspicuous absence, or why she would choose to have the ceremony downriver from the city in which they all lived.

There was a backup plan involving the local justice of the peace, though it seems likely that he would have been familiar with either the Wards or the Mitchells. There was no third option. By all accounts, they were confident they could marry in Memphis and then light out for St. Louis, where they would live happily ever after.

Alice was convinced that they would succeed. She had not proposed in three separate letters, reiterating her terms, out of sheer excitement. There had been too many misunderstandings between them, too many volatile elements; Alice wanted to make sure Freda took their commitment seriously this time. In each letter, she made it clear that there was no going back.

If Freda broke off their engagement, Alice promised to kill her for it.

CHAPTER FOUR

PRICE THE PISTOLS

BY JULY, THERE WAS TROUBLE. Amid their post-engagement euphoria, plans for the future took shape, but their reality remained the same, and so did their behavior. Alice was still jealous and possessive, and Freda as flirtatious as ever.

Ashley Roselle, a twenty-three-year-old postmaster from Featherstone, Arkansas, was not the first man to court Freda, but he seemed to be the most serious. And Freda, despite being involved in a clandestine marriage plot with another, did nothing to resist his overtures. If anything, the photograph and letters she sent Ashley's way did much to quicken his pursuit.

Even with eighty miles between them, Alice was no fool. Whenever she visited Golddust, she met as many of Freda's new friends and neighbors as possible, with an eye toward recruiting informants. Back home, she would write to them, as well as to those she had not met but knew of. She wanted to ascertain their impressions of Freda, and find out whether she was being courted by yet more suitors. In Memphis, Alice exploited chance encounters with people who knew Freda for potentially damning scraps of intelligence. There was no guile in her investigative approach, no attempt at artifice or reserve; she openly advanced on anyone who might have information.

It did not take long for Alice to learn about Ashley Roselle, and to make her displeasure known. Freda responded with her usual ambivalence; a dash of concern, a pinch of regret, but in the end, she was always an incorrigible flirt. In a letter to her betrothed, Freda callously reviewed her love for multiple suitors and reminded Alice of her desire to be onstage, yet another threat to their life together—all the while promising lifelong fidelity.

SAWDUST, TENN., July 11, 1891
Sunday Afternoon

My True Sweetheart, YBYR

I will start your letter this afternoon so I can write you a long one. I have still got the blues. Sweet love, you know that I love you better than anyone in the wide world. I am trying not to love others, and when I stop loving "A" and "H", I will tell you. I know that you are awfully jealous, sweet, but try not to be. Allie, do you mean that if I make you worse jealous you will hate me? For God's sake, Allie, don't ever hate me, for I believe it would kill me if you did. You don't know how much I worship you, sweetheart. Alvin, please be perfectly happy when you marry me, for I am true to you, and always will be forever. Maybe other women are not happy when they love others beside their husbands, but I will be perfectly happy when I become Mrs. Alvin J. Hard. I know you would do anything for me, loved one, for you love me. Sweetheart, I am not half as crazy to go on the stage as I was. When I marry you I will be happy and satisfied without going on the stage. I want to be with you all the time, for I more than love you. Good-bye until tomorrow.

SING

The whole courtship process seemed to be a game of youthful dalliance that Freda greatly enjoyed; proposals were like trophies, accolades she enthusiastically accepted without seriously considering what came after. And yet, Freda continually assured Alice—or rather, Alvin J. Ward, her fiancé—that their marriage would inspire fidelity, and she would embrace the virtues of true womanhood. Freda blithely encouraged the transition, never truly grasping the peril the terms of their engagement put her in.

As proof of sincerity, Freda enclosed a copy of a letter she had supposedly sent to Ashley.

Golddust, Tenn., July 1891

Mr. Ashley Roselle, Featherstone, Ark.:

Friend Ashley – I suppose you will be somewhat surprised when you receive this missive, but I write to ask you to forgive me for the way I have treated you. My friend, Alvin Ward, knew you had my picture. He was jealous and asked me to let him write for it and I did so. I knew I did you wrong and I don't blame you for tearing the picture up, but I do blame you for telling Dr. Vance and all the men on the boat about it. If you are my friend at all, please don't tell any one else. If you forgive me, write and say so; if not send my letter back. Remember, Ashley, I don't BEG you to forgive me. I merely ASK you to address

Your friend, SERG. JUeQ.
334 Vance st.
Memphis, Tenn.

True to form, Freda followed a gesture meant to quell jealousy with one that immediately inflamed it. It just so happened that Ashley was sure to be at a picnic Freda had also planned on attending. She promised, as if her word were reliable, that she would not speak to him—despite admitting to loving him.

"I will stop," she assured Alice in a letter, "I will always be true to you hereafter." Marriage, Freda promised, would fix all of their problems.

MEMPHIS, TENN., Aug. 1, 1891

YBIR:—Dearest Love—If you only knew it, you are getting me in trouble. I have stood it long enough. I am too jealous. I love you, Fred, and would kill Ashley before I would see him take you from me. You think I am only saying that for fun, but I really mean it. I know you love him, but if you would tell me the truth about it and wouldn't be so mean I would not be so jealous.

I have done something and I know you will get mad at me for it, but I can't help it. As long as you do me this way I will keep it up. Please be true to me, Sing, and I won't do anything wrong as long as you are true to me. I don't mean to do Ashley any harm, but if you still make me j— and deceive me I will. I hate to do it, but you will be the cause of it. He has done nothing to me, but I am mad with jealousy.

I am writing tonight, for I may go over to Lill's tomorrow evening. I can't write much for it is late. After this I will write only when I get a letter from my Sing.

Sweet one, you have done me mean, but I love you still with all your faults. I wish we were married, but it will be best for us to wait until next winter, unless you say no. We can get off all right, then, and take all the clothes or anything else we want. I won't write any more tonight, but will try to write more some time tomorrow.

I love you. I love you.

Sunday Evening - I wish I could see "Lovey." If I could squeeze you just once it would do me good. I wish you knew how I love you. I would give anything for you. I more than love you. Be sure and tell me when Miss Ada will let you come. If it is too long, run off. for I am afraid some boy will take you from me if we wait too long. You are so changeable. Fred, do you love me one-half as much as you did the first winter? I believe you loved me truer then than you ever did. You didn't fall in love with every boy that talked sweet to you then.

We went to see Miss Ward at 319 Georgia street yesterday. She wasn't there, but we sprinkled her woodhouse, and Lill drank some of her water out of her new hydrant. I took a piece of ivy and some slips of rose bushes. The pink one is gone. Water was standing in the yard. I wish my little sweetheart was living there now. Then I would have some one to kiss. I thought of how you loved me when you lived there. Sing, I don't do a thing but have the blues all the time. I am always thinking of you, and crying. You don't know how I hated to leave you on that day. I knew you would write that as soon as I left, and I was thinking about it the whole time you was on the boat. When were in the pilot-house I put my arm around you and you told me to take it away. I suppose you were thinking of some one else and wanted his arm around you. I know you were disappointed because he was not on the boat. I knew as soon as I heard what you told Lill that you didn't care for me, and you were deceiving me. If you don't love me you needn't but I will love you forever. I worship you love. I hope you will be true to me after this, but it is no use, as long as you think of Ashley and Harry so much. If you loved me as you say you do you would deceive them instead of me. I will try not to fuss at you any more, love, unless you say something about that until I see you. Do you remember what I said I would do if you would deceive me? That's what I was coming for, sweet one, honest; but Lill begged me. I love you, Fred, and hate to do it. Be true to me, will you, love? I had the nerve to price the pistols. They only had one size, and that was too

big. That was all that kept me from getting it. They were $12. Then I went for Lill and if it hadn't been for her I would have tried every place in Memphis until I got the right one. I didn't know what I was doing, Fred, if you only knew how I love you! Please try to stop loving them before you marry me, love. Nothing could make me happier than to have you love no one but me. If you loved me one-third as much as I do you I would feel better. I am so f—, I will ask you once more, for my last time, to desert all for my sake: even Ashley and Harry, and be true to me from this on forever. It is the last time I will ask it of you. If you love me you will do it. You can't love all at once, and love them truly. You will have to give up some. Will you have me? I have always been your friend. I am not merely your friend, but your true lover. I have done nothing to you, as I know of, to make you do me this way. I have always been true to you. You might think enough of me to tell me the truth once.
Yours forever.

SWEETHEART

But their marriage would solve nothing if it never came to pass, and this Ashley Roselle was a direct threat to their future. Since Freda could not be trusted, Alice went to meet this romantic rival herself—twice.

Ashley would later testify that Alice seemed unwell during their conversations, and that she had threatened to harm herself. The long, menacing letter that followed certainly suggested as much. She knew Freda would disapprove of the visits, but she reasoned she had every right to make them. To Alice's mind, Freda had made a commitment, and her infidelities warranted reprisal.

Ashley would have to die.

These were more than just words. Before picking up Lillie for one of their afternoon buggy rides, Alice went downtown alone, with just one goal in mind: She wanted to buy a gun.

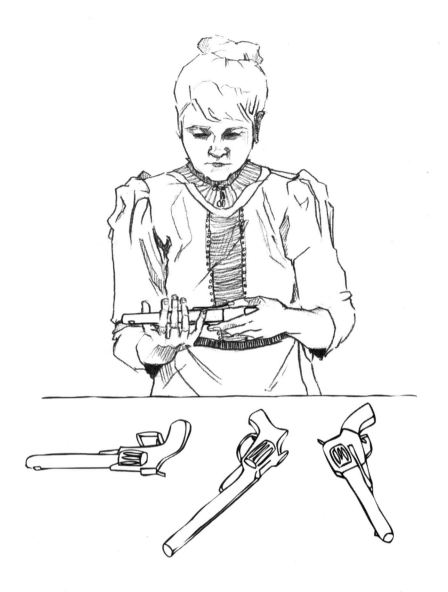

And what would stop her? She had the money, and the right. The pistol was a few dollars less than Freda's engagement ring, and there were no laws prohibiting a white woman from buying a firearm. The purchase was thwarted by a mere technicality: The guns were all too big. Had any of them been the right size, and had she not been due to fetch Lillie, Alice would have brought a gun home that day.

Alice returned home empty handed, but the trip was not a loss. She had illustrated, yet again, the deadly sincerity of her intentions. Despite the growing body of evidence, it seems Freda understood lethal threats to be a part of Alice's ardent manner of speech. Even as the situation devolved and Alice's plans became concrete, Freda refused to take her words seriously.

With love weighing heavily on her mind that day, Alice visited more than just purveyors of pistols. She brought Lillie to 319 George Street, to the house Freda had called home in Memphis. Had she still lived there, Alice wrote, she could kiss her, but her visit was instead spent gloomily meandering around the property, collecting ivy and picking roses.

Burdened by desperation, Alice's anger deepened into hopeless melancholy. The long, tortured ruminations in her letter were but a sampling of the thoughts that oppressed her. We will never know exactly how or when Alice and Freda fell in love, but the letter suggests it happened at Miss Higbee's, when chumming turned into something much more. But now her beloved was fading away. Did Freda love Alice half as much as when she lived on George Street?

"You didn't fall in love with every boy that talked sweet to you then," she wrote. Other suitors had never been a real concern, but Alice saw these new romantic rivals as more than just competition. Freda admitted to *loving* them, even as she claimed to love Alice best.

Alice could not fathom entertaining other prospects; Freda was her one and only. It was getting harder to deny that her feelings for Freda were stronger than Freda's feelings for her. In letters, Alice seemed to hope that drawing attention to this disparity might solicit comforting protestations, or perhaps she hoped it would inspire Freda to stop "loving" these other men *before* they married. But Freda consistently failed to rise to the occasion.

When Alice visited 319 George Street that day, she went in search of a phantom—the old Freda Ward, resident of Memphis, student at Miss Higbee's, sweetheart of Alice Mitchell.

On August 1, 1891, Alice sent the lengthy letter to the new Freda Ward, resident of Golddust, a student of nowhere, a sweetheart to many. If their elopement succeeded, Freda would likely leave her sister's home before it arrived—but for all Alice knew, Ashley Roselle or some other suitor in Golddust was, at that very moment, tempting Freda away.

Unbeknownst to Alice, two letters were en route from Freda's home to the Mitchell residence that very same day, by way of her older brother, Robert, and they confirmed her greatest fear.

Someone had indeed come between them—but it wasn't Ashley Roselle.

CHAPTER FIVE

I THOUGHT YOU WERE A LADY

AFTER MONTHS OF REHEARSAL, Freda's cue had finally come. On that summer night in 1891, she was, for once it seemed, fully committed to playing her role. She took supper with her family in Golddust as if it were any other meal, and then retired to bed, as she had so many nights before.

But once inside her room, Freda did not shed her clothing from the day, nor satisfy more than perfunctory ablutions. She was waiting for the moment—between ten o'clock and two in the morning—when the steamer would announce itself, confident that her performance that night had fooled everyone.

But as it turned out, Freda was not the only actress in the Ward family.

Ada Volkmar had also acted her way through their nightly ritual. And now, as Freda waited inside her bedroom for the steamer, Ada did the exact same thing just outside of it.

When their mother died in 1882, the eldest Ward sister was expected to assume her duties, and Ada had done her best for Jo and Freda.[11] But she was married now, and with the move up to Golddust, her focus had shifted on to her own household, which included at least one boarder. Thomas Ward had followed, youngest daughters in tow. Since new business opportunities kept him busy, Jo and Freda once again fell under Ada's purview, moving in with her and her husband, William Volkmar.

Back in Memphis, Ada had noticed that Alice and Freda had grown very close. The Ward home had been but one backdrop for their relationship, interspersed with visits to the Mitchell and Johnson home, Miss Higbee's, the many trips downtown, and the buggy rides.

But the move to Golddust initiated bouts of forced physical separation followed by lengthy visits, and offered Ada a front row seat to Alice and Freda's conspicuous affection. She had seen girls chumming around Memphis, and Jo and Lillie regarded each other with particular warmth, but those romantic friendships looked increasingly tepid when compared to Alice and Freda.

Ada would later testify that she developed a strong aversion to their tender embraces, the constant kissing and fawning. But even so, the romantic charge that she witnessed was in no sense *meaningful* to her. Like most Americans in the nineteenth century, Ada had no explanation for what she was seeing. And thus it was dismissed as merely frivolous, if not irritating excess.

In fact, with Freda occupied, Ada had one less thing to worry about. She had welcomed Alice into her home for days at a time, and happily sent Freda down to visit the Mitchells in Memphis. Besides, Ada had never seen Alice act in an improper fashion, flirt with men, or wear inappropriate clothing, and there were no rumors to suggest otherwise. Alice was a lady, and her family, headed by the beloved "Uncle George," was respected in Memphis.

She may have continued to unwittingly enable their plans had she not, by chance, caught a glimpse of Freda's letters. The girls wrote often enough

that the family limited them to two letters a week, but Ada was not so naïve as to ignore the many more that came and went. Alice and Freda were fond of pseudonyms and pet names, but all of the letters originated in the same cities, and were addressed by the same hands. Ada had probably regarded the excessive correspondence as the silly preoccupation of two young women, out of school but not yet wed, with little to do, spending their free time filling letters with gossip about former classmates or ads in the matrimonial paper.

But once Ada actually read the letters in their entirety, they revealed, in near chronological order, that Alice and Freda were doing something altogether different than chumming. They were corresponding as lovers would, using the kinds of words and sentiments Ada had likely exchanged with her own husband during their courtship. Why would two women be making such professions to each other? It made no sense to her—but that was not the most pressing issue.

As Ada discovered, Freda intended to sneak out of her own home that very night, marry Alice in Memphis, and light out for St. Louis. Ada had never read a similar tale in the papers, but she had read plenty of harrowing, moralistic tales about sheltered young women who thrust themselves into the world, only to be overwhelmed by its treachery. In these published stories, mothers were almost always depicted as careless, blind to the shameful schemes unfolding in their domestic sphere, while the men, once informed, would sprint out into the world as saviors, unrelenting in their gallant effort to preserve familial honor.

If the young woman was found, it was likely to be in a brothel, or under the influence of an unseemly man not dissimilar to George Wickham, the charming officer who convinces Lydia Bennett to run away with him in Jane Austen's 1813 novel, *Pride and Prejudice*. Wickham had no intention of actually marrying Lydia, but Mr. Darcy used his powers of persuasion, or more specifically, his massive fortune, to tempt him into decency. But few had such means and power, and the Wards were definitely not among them. Besides, if these rescue attempts were at all successful, the young woman's return was hardly triumphant. Her reputation was tarnished, and that tainted her entire family.

For his part, William Volkmar was sure there was a "Wickham" laying in wait. No matter how many times Ada explained that Alice and Freda planned to marry *each other*, he insisted there was a man at the bottom of it. Surely Ada had misunderstood, and Alice was actually just an accessory in some unscrupulous man's master plan. And so he spent that summer evening on the porch, Winchester rifle in hand, waiting for an unnamed miscreant who would dare pluck a chaste young lady from his respectable home.

And that was the scene in Golddust, with all three waiting in different places in and around the house, with differing ideas of what was going on, when the moment finally came. The boat cued its arrival with a whistle, which meant Freda, still fully clothed, was surely picking up her valise. William had heard it, too, but kept watching for a man to materialize. It was dark, but there was no rustling underfoot, no nasally sound of horses breathing. Unwilling to risk his wife's ire if her youngest sister slipped out undetected, William was forced to quit his post, and headed toward his sister-in-law's bedroom.

ADA WOULD HAVE NO MORE OF ALICE MITCHELL. After she recovered from the previous night's theatrics—confronting Freda, and then interrogating her—Ada penned two letters to the Mitchells in Golddust, only one of which had Alice's name on it.

GoldDust, Tenn., Aug.¹ 1891

Miss Allie Mitchell:

Ere now you must fully realize that your supposed well laid plans to take Fred away have all gone awry. You should have taken into consideration that Fred had a sister watching over her who had good eyes and plenty of common sense, and was fully competent to take care of her sister. I return your "engagement ring" as you called it, and all else that I know of your having sent Fred, as you won't marry her yet awhile. Don't try in any way, shape, form or manner to have any intercourse with Fred again. I thought you were a lady. I have found out to the contrary. Stay at home and attend to your own business, and Fred will do likewise. I hope you will live to see the day that you will realize how very foolish such proceedings were.

MRS. W. H. VOLKMAR

P.S. — I enclose $2.40 all I can find out that Fred owes you. $1.75 for the dress and 50 cents for the harp and 15 cents that you sent to pay the porter for the ring. If she owes you any more, please let me know and I will send it to you.

MRS. W. H. V

The other letter was sent to Isabella Mitchell, Alice's mother. Even though the circumstances were dire and demanded urgent attention, there was a protocol in polite society, and such domestic dramas fell under the purview of maternal authority. It had been Ada's choice to tell her husband, but it was not her place to speak directly with Alice's father. She had not even sent it directly to the Mitchell residence, but rather to Alice's older brother, Robert, who safely delivered them to the family home.

If nothing else, Ada expected to be taken at her word. It was a bizarre tale for the turn-of-the-century, but the stakes were high enough that it surely warranted redress. Isabella read the letter, and made its contents known to her youngest daughter.

Alice adopted a mostly passive stance, playing the obedient daughter averse to scandal. It was the obvious choice, given that Isabella spoke of things Alice had never dared to write. Ada's letter was brimming with intimate details that could only have come from Freda. Her fiancé had cracked under pressure, making neither any effort to protect her confidences with Alice, nor any attempt to preserve the possibility of a future together.

It now seemed prescient that Alice had, in the past, suggested to Isabella that Ada was not well. The letter she sent to Alice's mother seemed so far-fetched, so bold and out of touch with reality, that even Isabella concluded Ada must have "grossly exaggerated and misunderstood the matter."[12] Of course, Alice did nothing to disabuse her mother of this interpretation, nor did she argue against Isabella's verdict, the same one imposed by Ada.

Alice and Freda were never to speak again.

CHAPTER SIX

YOU TOLD AND I DID TOO

ALICE HAD NO INTENTION OF keeping away from Freda. Though interception was all but guaranteed, she posted a confused letter just a few days after the foiled elopement. Alice filled the page with blame, regret, and just a bit of hope, before requesting one final meeting.

MEMPHIS, TENN., Aug. 7, 1891

Dear Fred- As Miss Ada sent my things back I will return yours all except the picture. I WONT part with that. I told mama and she said I could keep that. If there is anything else I have let me know and I will send it.

Remember, Fred, there is no hard feeling toward you on my side. They have turned you against me, although I know you did not think as much of me as you said you did. You did it only to save your life. When I first asked you to marry me I gave you a chance to think and say no. You wrote and said yes in three letters before I said for certain you had promised. I told you then to think what we were risking, but you still said you would be mine. After that I wouldn't let you break the engagement. I not merely begged you to marry me, but I forced you. I am sorry I have gotten you in trouble, "Sing," but I beg you to forgive me. Mr. and Mrs. Volkmar opened our letters unknown to us and have turned you against me. Of course, I don't ask you to marry me after this, for if they would miss us it would be worse than ever. I have told everything to mama. You told and I did too. I even told her about you running off and going on the stage with Harry, and about Ashley asking you to marry him and you had Ashley's ring and all. You said if it wasn't for me you would have been Mrs. Roselle. I suppose it would have been better in the end. If they give you this letter it will be the last I will write. If I could see you just once it would be all I would want. I have one thing to ask you. After that you needn't even speak to me.

I will forgive you for writing that letter to Ashley. I forgive you for everything you have done.

Please do me a favor, and that is destroy every letter I have ever written to you. Don't let this cause hard feelings between you and Lil, for she had nothing to do with it. I LOVE YOU STILL and will forever. Will you forgive me? Please answer and I won't write any more or have anything else to do with you, for your sake.

Yours forever, ALLIE

There would be no response from Freda. She would not grant Alice her final request to meet in person. And as Alice would learn in just a few months time, when much of America would clamor for it, Freda most certainly did not destroy their letters.

WHEN A MONTH PASSED WITH NO WORD, Alice became convinced that Freda had not received her final plea, or that if she had, that her attempts to respond had been thwarted by others. The possibility that Freda herself had chosen not to reply to a letter full of accusations, or that Freda may have found relief in Ada's intervention, never seemed to register with Alice.

This time, Alice would be more careful. Her solution was to mask the next letter's origin by sending it first to Chicago, where it would then be rerouted to Golddust. This circuitous route would be prominently stamped on the envelope, but just in case the subterfuge was detected by watchful eyes, Alice took the additional precaution of writing not as herself, but as her alter ego, "Freda Myra Ward."

Chicago, Ill., Aug. 30, 1891

Dear Freddie:

I know you will be surprised when you get this, for it was reported that I was dead, but I am still alive. I am all right now. Better than I have ever felt. Rob Ritchie was in New York at the same time I was, and when he heard I was not expected to live he said I was dead.

They thought I was dying and gave me up in July, and that is when he said I was dead. I don't thank him one bit for it. I was only supposed to be dead. I hope you will soon go to Memphis and meet the dead girl. I will go next week. It is too changeable here for me. How long did Alice and Lillie stay at the wonderful city of Golddust?

I know you enjoyed their visit. I passed there on the boat while they were there, but I did not see any of you. I suppose you were out viewing the wonderful city or calling on the great people. Hoping you are not angry with me for not writing before, I remain your friend,

FREDA M. WARD

Address general delivery C. S., Memphis, Tenn.
P.S. - I will be there before your letter will.

At this point, the true meaning of this thinly veiled letter was easily discernible to anyone privy to their foiled elopement—and most certainly to Ada. July, the month the signer notes "they thought I was dying," was the very month their plan died through discovery. It was also the season that, vis-à-vis maternal orders, their love was supposed to die, too. "I will be there before your letter will," Alice concludes, as if to say, just come, my love, no need to send a letter ahead of time. At least on that point, Freda would acquiesce—there would be no letter posted in return.

ALICE SPENT THE MONTH OF SEPTEMBER as she had August, her heartbreak on full display. She often withdrew from the Mitchell family during the day, and when she did appear, it was in an abject state, her eyes watering, her expression absent and forlorn. At night, while the rest of the family slept, she lay awake, indulging her sorrow. She often refused the food she was served, and completely avoided the dining table whenever possible. Her shapely figure began to waste away.

When she left her bedroom, it was most often for the kitchen, to unearth the locked box. She spent hours perusing its contents, touching the photograph of Freda, fingering the returned engagement ring. She mostly reread letters, and for just a moment, however briefly, she would lose herself in a memory. A smile would spread across her face, perhaps a laugh even escaping her lips.

Alice was rarely alone in the kitchen. But she liked the family's cook, Lucy Franklin, who often brought along her own six-year-old child, a much needed diversion for Alice.

Lucy would later testify that the Mitchells mistreated their youngest, though she could not specify how. She understood the kitchen, her work-space, to be a refuge for Alice, a place where she could receive the compassion so sorely lacking in the rest of the house. And Lucy listened to Alice's tale of woe, even though it was filled with half-truths. She assumed that Alice's ex-fiancé was a man, and Alice never corrected her. And for whatever reason, Alice blamed the broken engagement on her own sisters, not Ada. Though Lucy may have been in the dark on many of the details, she seemed to understand the most important part, the heartbreak and suffering.

Alice was not right in her mind, Lucy would later testify. Her eyes shone with a strange luster, others would say. And some of what they would recall from that time was actually true, and very odd indeed.

When coal was delivered to the house, Alice did not sign the receipt in her own name, or that of her mother or father. Instead, she wrote out the name Freda Ward in careful script. The receipts would later serve as evidence, and both the defense and prosecution questioned Alice about the aberration. She would admit to having signed Freda's name not once, but on *five* separate occasions, only to claim that she had not realized what she was doing. How could she explain something she did not remember?

"I was thinking of Freda," she would later testify. It would be her answer to most questions.

When it came to her father's razor, however, Alice's memory was perfectly intact. She confessed that she had stolen it on the first of November.

The razor's absence had not gone unnoticed. George Mitchell looked for it in his bedroom, and throughout the house. He asked his sons if they had taken it, and questioned the rest of the family.

It was becoming clear to Alice that each passing day brought her closer to the inevitable. Freda would leave for good, and they would never meet again. The Wards were determined to keep the young women apart, to encourage Freda to live a different life, to love another person. Alice had always known that this might happen, and that she would not be able to stand it. She would not stand for it, and had promised Freda as much.

And so, she carried the razor around every day in her dress pocket, just in case Freda came to town. It was only later that Alice's father realized, yes, of course, Alice had left the room whenever he asked if anyone had seen it.

BY DECEMBER, Alice was desperate for news of Freda. No one seemed to have anything new to offer. Jo had also abruptly cut off communication with Lillie, which, because Lillie had been ignorant of Alice and Freda's engagement, seemed inexplicable to her.

Lillie was sad to lose the Wards and see their quartet dismantled, but for Alice, the loss was devastating. Eager to lighten her mood, Lillie readily agreed to Alice's requests, even penning a letter to Ashley Roselle on her behalf. She had been listening to Alice pine about Freda's silence, never grasping the full meaning of it, but this request, Lillie would later explain, made perfect sense to her. It seemed no different than the inconsequential letters they had sent in the past, to men they had met on the electric car line and found in the pages of the matrimonial paper. But no matter how much Lillie tried, no matter how much she praised and flattered Ashley, Alice seemed unsatisfied with the letters, and soon enough, Lillie was told to stop writing them.

Alice would write the letters herself. In December, and then again in January, Alice sent the man she considered her romantic nemesis hand-written pages crammed with flattering, amorous sentiments. She confessed feelings for him she did not have, and admired attributes she likely loathed, in order to gauge Ashley's commitment to Freda. She even requested to meet him in person, on the *Rosa Lee*, when he came through Memphis. But while he agreed to talk to her on the steamer, it was out of mere civility. When they met, Ashley did not return her affections, or tell her anything of worth about his relationship with Freda.

And that was how 1892 began for Alice Mitchell.

The new year had shown little promise when, in January, it finally happened: Freda arrived in Memphis. The news electrified Alice when she happened upon it, and it propelled her into action.

Of course, Alice knew that Freda could not stay with her. She assumed—with all the confidence of delusion—that Ada's vigilance was the only reason Freda had not sent word ahead of the visit. But none of that mattered. Alice was overcome by the one fact that did matter: Freda was nearby.

Alice knew Freda loved to be courted, so she sent not one, but two letters to Mrs. Kimbrough's house on Hernando Street. As luck would have it, Ada had stayed back in Golddust, which allowed Alice to hope that Jo, who had once been a dear friend to her and Lillie, might allow them to meet.

Alice longed for a reply, but wasted no time waiting around for one. Whenever she could manage an outing in the increasingly harsh January weather, Alice drove her buggy by Hernando Street. A moment to talk, to be alone, would be ideal, but she would settle for very little at that point.

Which is probably why she felt oddly encouraged when one of her letters was sent back to the Mitchell household. All it took was Freda's hand-

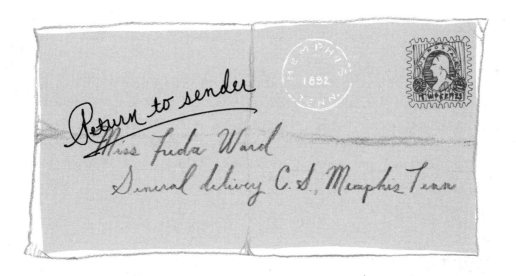

writing, marking the envelope to be returned, for Alice to grow hopeful.

Finally, after so many failed attempts, she spotted Freda alone on the street. Alice watched her beloved go into a photograph gallery, and waited outside, her heart no doubt pounding, the blood coursing through her veins, the excitement warming her body.

But when Freda finally exited, she did not stop to speak to Alice, or wink, or give any sign of recognition. Freda walked right past Alice as if she were just another stranger on a busy downtown street, her eyes fixed ahead, and then she disappeared into Mrs. Carroll's home.

Alice thrust her trembling hands into her dress pockets, but the shock of the interaction, of having been completely ignored, rendered her fingers too unsteady to retrieve the razor, much less use it. She could have waited for Freda to head back to Mrs. Kimbrough's house, but she went home instead. Had she misunderstood the encounter? Maybe Freda had not seen her at all, or thought Alice was out of town, and would make contact soon. And then, finally, Freda did just that.

Alice must have been brimming with hope when the envelope arrived, to see Freda's own handwriting intended for her, after so many months of

MEMPHIS, TENN., Jan. 17, 1772

DEAR ALLIE:

I love you now and always will, but I have been
forbidden ... to speak to you and I have to obey. You say I am
as much to blame as you are. If I have done you any harm
or caused you any trouble, I humbly beg your forgiveness. Please
don't let any one know I wrote this. No one knows about that
last summer's business except our family, that is unless you
have told some one. We go back to Golddust this evening.

FREDA

absolute silence. She probably felt relief, and took the unopened letter as confirmation that they were still in love, and always would be.

But the letter conveyed a disquieting message. Freda intended to obey Ada. She was *choosing* to follow rules set by another. This was exactly the kind of obedience Alice had repeatedly demanded of Freda, but never fully received. It seemed to suggest that she had not been Freda's true love at all, but rather just another suitor to trifle with, and then discard as easily as the others. How could Freda have so dismissively referred to their engagement as "last summer's business?" Freda was ashamed. She truly wanted their history to be erased, as if it had never happened.

However, Alice saw a glimmer of hope, a hint at the end of the letter. Surely Freda would not have divulged her departure had she not wanted Alice to see her off. Still, it seemed odd. Everyone knew the steamers had altered their schedule on account of the inclement weather; the ship Freda claimed to be leaving on was no longer scheduled to leave that night. Was it possible that Freda did not know that, even though she was staying at the widow Kimbrough's house, so close to the waterfront? The comings and goings of ships were conspicuous enough that any aberration in the schedule became the subject of small talk in town. Even Alice, who hardly spoke to anyone anymore, knew the next departure was not for days.

Nonetheless, when the next departure time did arrive, Alice picked up Lillie in the buggy, and went down to the dock. Lillie believed they were saying good-bye, that there had been some kind of reconciliation, and thought nothing of boarding the boat and helping Alice search for the Wards.

They walked the length of the steamer, making inquiries all along the way. But the sisters were nowhere to be found. As the ship departed, leaving the Wards behind in Memphis, everything became clear.

MEMPHIS, Tenn., Jan. 21, 1892

Fred – Send me my photo, which you have that was taken with Estelle. Also send me the silver ring that I gave you. Maybe you think I believe you left Memphis Monday. You knew as well as I did that the steamer Rosa Lee was not running regular. I suppose you will go home on the Ora Lee tomorrow, or wait for the Rosa Lee Monday.

Don't let any one know you wrote to me! If you trouble me any more I will not only let any one know, but will send the letter to Mrs. W. H. Volkmar, and something else, too. Do you remember who you met on Union street, near Hernando street, this afternoon? I heard more scandal about Mr. — and Mrs. — that kept the saloon on Poplar street, near Front Row today.

7 Madison street.　　　　ALLIE

Alice's message to Freda seemed clear: You may try to deceive me by switching steamers, but I will haunt the docks until I find you. The final lines are mysterious, but may be an allusion to their last meeting on the street, when Alice's ex-fiancé had walked right past her.

It would be the last letter she ever sent Freda, and she had already received the last one Freda would ever send to her. Alice was carrying it around in her dress pocket, where it would remain until January 25, 1892. By the time the police took it from her, it was covered in the writer's own blood.

PART II

A MOST
SHOCKING CRIME

CHAPTER SEVEN

EROTOMANIA

LESS THAN AN HOUR AFTER THE MURDER, Memphis's Chief of Police knocked on the front door of the Mitchell's fashionable home on Union Street. Chief Davis was sorry to disturb "Uncle George," as the retired salesman was affectionately called, and sorrier still for the decidedly unpleasant nature of the call. He had come to arrest George Mitchell's youngest daughter for the murder of Freda Ward.

George had been expecting him. He readied himself and Alice for a trip to the jailhouse, just a few minute's walk from the scene of the crime. He waited patiently as Davis booked his nineteen-year-old daughter on the charge of murder, amiably chatting with jailers, all sympathetic friends who promised to look after Alice while he sought legal representation.

By eight o'clock that evening, George returned with two of the most prominent, expensive attorneys in Eastern Tennessee, if not the entire state. Both Colonel George Gantt and General Luke Wright were affluent, respectable Memphians from old, Southern families. They had emerged as community leaders after a series of yellow fever outbreaks in the 1870s all

General Luke Wright   Colonel George Gantt

but ruined the city; Memphis's charter was revoked, the economy stalled, and its population dwindled, with thousands buried and many more having fled, never to return.[13]

Col. Gantt was considered Memphis's preeminent litigator, peerless in legal research and unrivaled in courtroom debate. The firm that bore his name was a breeding ground for high level political and business leaders, whose power and wealth gave them an extraordinary degree of influence in the South.

Gen. Wright, son of a Tennessee Supreme Court Justice, had a distinct advantage in the case. His title was honorific, bestowed upon him for a commendable job as attorney general in Shelby County, where the Mitchell-Ward case would be heard. He would go on to collect far more titles in his career, serving as the first United States Ambassador to Japan, and then as Secretary of War under President Theodore Roosevelt.

Despite the defense's legal prowess, it was George Mitchell, and not the lawyers he hired, who determined Alice's plea. It was not the first time he had peremptorily imposed a diagnosis in his family. George had placed his wife, Isabella in the hospital after she gave birth at home—three times—deeming what was likely postpartum depression as behavior unsuitable for a wife and mother.[14]

On the very night Alice had slashed a seventeen-year-old woman's throat, her father convinced two formidable lawyers that his daughter could not be tried for murder. There was no denying that she had killed Freda—Alice had already confessed, and there were plenty of witnesses—but in 1892, her motive was utterly inconceivable to them. Alice's insistence that she killed Freda because she loved her and could not stand the idea of anyone else having her, and that the young women had planned to marry, seemed nothing short of insane.

BY THE TIME GANTT AND WRIGHT EMERGED from Alice's cell that evening, they had an interview in hand and a plan of action.

No one outside of the judicial system would be allowed to speak to Alice, and those within it would be closely supervised. By denying access to their client, Gantt and Wright could carefully manage Alice's story, since any reports disseminated through the press could possibly set the tone for the entire trial.

Their first opportunity to steer the public narrative presented itself the moment Alice's newly formed defense team exited the jailhouse. News of a well-to-do white woman turned murderess were rapidly circulating through Memphis. Gawkers and journalists alike had already begun swarming outside of the building, desperate for any information about what was rumored to have been—to use what would become one of their favorite words for the case—an *unnatural* crime. They were desperate to hear Alice's side of the story, and happy to accept the version Gantt and Wright were peddling. And the defense was more than happy to see the press and spectators repeat what they had heard as if it were firsthand account, as if they had heard the words spoken by Alice herself.

But Gantt and Wright had no intention of giving them the whole statement that night. Borrowing from a publishing format usually reserved for works of fiction, they serialized Alice's interview, releasing it in bits and pieces over the next few days, keeping reporters and readers tantalized and hungry for more. The defense made good use of the time in-between the daily publication, seeking out a team of medical experts to add weight to the plea they hoped to file—present insanity—and all in time to be printed in the next installment.

Gantt and Wright were no strangers to mass media. They understood the public's bottomless desire for sensational news stories, especially for crimes of passion. They correctly anticipated that the Mitchell case, a cornucopia of scandalous detail, would attract unprecedented attention. The inescapable din of news reports, gossip, and fervent speculation would surely reach the ears of potential jurors.

Steering the press's narrative was also the quickest way to get to Judge Julius DuBose, who presided over all the cases in the jailhouse. It was easy enough to predict he would turn to the *Memphis Public Ledger* first. Not only had he started his career as an editor at the *Public Ledger*, but the paper had the clear advantage over all the other outlets: It was the first, longest

Memphis Appeal Avalanche .... JUDGE JULIUS DUBOSE

MEMPHIS PUBLIC LEDGER .... COLONEL GEORGE GANTT

Memphis Commercial .... GENERAL LUKE WRIGHT

running, and most popular evening paper in Memphis. If any newspapers were going to influence the judge, it would be the *Public Ledger*. The reports and editorials in the paper not only had the potential to spin their own version of the latest details in the case, but more importantly, serve as a daily performance review of the judge himself. It was possible that, after reading the nightly paper, Judge DuBose would take its opinions into consideration as much as the evidence presented in court.

In 1892, there were more than a dozen papers in Memphis, all of which were owned by local white men who wielded power in various realms.[15] This was business as usual in the press; even Wright, just a few years earlier, had gladly stepped up as one of the first investors in the *Memphis Commercial*. Powerful Memphians backed their pet publications in order to further their business, personal, and political agendas. These competing factions modeled themselves after New York's lucrative, mass circulation papers, where advertisers paid top dollar to appear next to a sensational story, in turn sending the newspapers' circulations soaring.[16]

This was certainly the practice of the *Public Ledger* and the *Commercial*. But to be truly successful in shaping opinions statewide—and as it would turn out, around the nation—Gantt and Wright would have to win over the *Memphis Appeal Avalanche*.

The *Appeal Avalanche* was the largest morning paper in the city, and made bold claims on the entire state of Tennessee. Though just a couple of years old, it possessed two things no other paper in Memphis had: a linotype machine and an exclusive deal with the Associated Press.[17] The linotype produced an entire line of metal type at once, a far more efficient and faster means of publishing than the old industry standard, the manual process of setting type letter-by-letter. The Associated Press was around forty years old by the time the *Appeal Avalanche* joined, and the news cooperative had enjoyed a legendary reputation for dramatically increasing the transmission of news across the country since the Civil War.

Just before midnight, local papers sent what little information they had about the murder of Freda Ward through the wire, and by morning, big urban dailies in major cities were already desperate for more. Nothing in Memphis had ever attracted such national interest, and thus none of the national, mass circulation papers had reporters stationed in the vicinity. As they scrambled to tap local journalists, the largest, most far-flung American newspapers, including the *New York World* and the *San Francisco Chronicle*, ordered their staff writers to board the next train to Tennessee.

IN THE DAYS THAT FOLLOWED THE MURDER, nearly every newspaper in the country eagerly printed fact alongside fiction, eschewing even the most basic research efforts in favor of speedy transmission. The out-of-towners were exempt from local redress, and those newspapers took liberties with even the smallest details. The *North American of Philadelphia* aged seventeen-year-old Freda to nineteen, and reported that the young women's estrangement began because "Freda's friends considered Miss Mitchell 'too fast.'"

The *New York Times* misspelled Lillie Johnson's first and last name, identifying her as "Lizzie Johnston," and offered a muddled timeline in which Alice first murdered Freda, and then cut Jo.[18] Memphis readers would have immediately questioned the article's sub-headline, in which the paper of record erroneously identified Alice as a "society girl." In the social hierarchy of the South, slave-owning families who had made millions in cotton and horse breeding were "familiar figures in society," not a merchant's daughter. Similarly, Freda, the daughter of a machinist who had sought greater prospects up river in Golddust—and came from a family that was far less well-to-do than the Mitchells—was not a member of Tennessee's semi-aristocratic class. Neither girl had made the guest lists at parties the

Memphis elite staged on their sprawling estates, many of which still operated as plantations.

But local newspapers specialized in their own brand of creative reporting, including embellishments that read more like popular fiction than true crime. Judge DuBose's former employer, the *Public Ledger*, described the murder scene with flourish:

> Grasping her by the hair Miss Mitchell pulled her head back, exposing the round, white throat. Again the keen razor was brought into play, and this time it did its work with frightful completeness. The girl was almost beheaded, and fell fainting to the ground, which was soon drenched with her rushing blood.[19]

The racial identifiers—the *New York Times* emphasized Freda's "white bosom" and the *Public Ledger* spoke of her "white throat"—were visceral scare tactics used to remind readers that these were the kind of people they knew and cared about.[20] Journalists knew that the story would be far less consequential to readers if the murderer and victim had been male, not white, or of lesser economic means. And if they could punctuate the scene with a subtly sexualized near-beheading, all the better.

To American readers in the 1890s, the most confusing part of the Mitchell case had little to do with inconsistent reporting. The early headlines emphasized how confounding the very idea of same-sex love was in the first place. Reporters relied heavily on words like "unnatural," "strange," and "perverted."

When all else failed, reporters attempted to explain that Alice was "a man" in the relationship. Though, they conceded, not masculine in her

The San Francisco Examiner
JANUARY 31, 1892.
LOVE RUNS MAD AND DEADLY, UNNATURAL PASSION... STEELED THE ARM OF ALICE MITCHELL

Memphis Appeal Avalanche
FEBRUARY 4, 1892.
"MISS ALICE MITCHELL'S LUNACY, COUNSEL HAVE CONFIDENCE THAT EROTOMANIA CAN BE ESTABLISHED, THE PERVERTED AFFECTION OF ONE GIRL FOR ANOTHER."

MEMPHIS PUBLIC LEDGER
JANUARY 26, 1892.
I LOVED HER SO!

NEW YORK WORLD
JANUARY 29, 1892. "BEGS TO SEE HER FREDA.... PASSIONATE LOVE LETTERS SUCH AS A MAN MIGHT WRITE."

The San Francisco Examiner
JANUARY 30, 1892.
"INVESTIGATING THE STORY OF STRANGE PASSION AND DEATH"

dress or countenance, her supposedly hidden proclivity toward all things male was yet another way reporters could contrast Alice with "normal" young women. In an interview with the *Appeal Avalanche*, Gantt explained that Alice had quietly, but consistently, defied gender norms her entire life:

. . . everything she has done, her peculiarities, whether during her infancy she played with dolls or other such toys in
which the average female delights, whether she had a fondness
for those of her own or the opposite sex, all of these will be circumstances going to show the state and quality of her mind.[21]

Newspapers enthusiastically accepted whatever scraps of information
the defense tossed at them, and relied on an abundance of loose-lipped
locals to fill in the gaps. The city was overtaken with intrigue, and there
were hordes of Memphians who wished to weigh in on the murder. Some
sought to correct erroneous material, but more often than not, they offered
subjective observations. These opinions were often based on personal experience with the Mitchells or the Wards, though as time went on, they were
clearly influenced by what they read in the newspapers, too. Others, whose
lack of connection to the case did not deter them from offering highly
quotable views and speculation, were also tapped as ongoing sources. These
unreliable perspectives were no more subject to fact checking than any of
the other details making their way across the nation.

Neighbor John Perry offered what was likely a nebulous recollection of
the Mitchell's youngest daughter, combined with what he had obviously
absorbed about the version of Alice now being discussed in newspapers as
an insane murderess.[22]

I live next door to Mr. George Mitchell and have known
Alice for nine years or more, and have never considered her
strong mentally. Her manner has been always flighty and
unsettled and her ways different from that of most girls. She
was of an impulsive disposition, and given to doing very much
as the present mood inclined her, whether it was to snatch up
a rifle and stand about her yard shooting sparrows or to ride

a bare back horse at break-neck speed about the premises. I have never seen anything about her conduct that was at all immodest, nor was she the least bit fast as regards to men. On the contrary, she seemed to care nothing for them and rather preferred the society of her own sex. . . . From a long and close knowledge of Alice Mitchell her act was that of an insane woman.[23]

Concerned citizens, and those with other sorts of motives, reached out to the authorities as well. The attorney general's office received many letters, both signed and anonymous, riddled with suspect details, outlandish claims, and transparent lies. While the offices of the court and the police privately dismissed the more outrageous reports, they were more than willing to turn around and discuss them with reporters. Attorney General George Peters was constantly asked about a popular rumor that Alice Mitchell had sent the office a letter from jail, but Peters shunned it as "the ebullition of a crank." Likewise, a Memphis detective relayed a phone call he received from an agitated man in Cincinnati who informed him that three years prior to Freda's murder, Alice had "made love like a man to his daughter, now deceased."[24]

Relentless messages concerning the supposed unnaturalness of Alice's motives were clearly working. In the mind of the public, she seemed endowed with an almost supernatural power to commit heinous acts, no matter the time or place.

THE PROSECUTION OFFERED very little information beyond stating that Alice was of sound mind—a decidedly insipid claim next to the defense's adamant plea; dramatic presentation of sensational, anecdotal "evidence"; and aggressive campaigning. Public opinion was leaning toward the defense, but Gantt and Wright had yet to play their wild card: the most incendiary part of Alice's statement.

The *Appeal Avalanche* published this part of Alice's statement under the headline, "WHO IS THIS JESSIE JAMES?"

The day of our wedding was set, and then not all of the powers in the world could have separated us. It was our intention to leave here and go to St. Louis, and I would have been Freda's slave. I would have devoted my whole life to making her happy.... But when Freda returned my engagement ring it broke my heart. It was the most cruel thing I had ever suffered. I could not bear the idea of being separated from her whom I loved more dearly than my life. I wrote to her and implored her to not to break off the engagement, but my letters availed nothing. I could not bear to think of her living in the company of others. Then, indeed, I resolved to kill Freda because I loved her so much that I wanted her to die loving me, and when she did die I know she loved me better than any other human being on earth. I got my father's razor and made up my mind to kill Freda, and now I know she is happy. [25]

Today's readers are likely to interpret this confession as the unfortunate saga of a troubled, teenage romance turned deadly: Alice believed she had found her one true love, and that their commitment could withstand any challenge—or be immortalized by death. For some time, Freda felt the same way, or at least proved convincing enough that the withdrawal of her affections truly broke Alice's heart. Her only solace was the assumption that Freda was bowing to familial pressure, and when she learned this was not the case, that Freda's love had been fickle, Alice was determined to hold her to their agreement. If any part of her statement casts a doubt on Alice's sanity, it is the conclusion, in which she claims to know Freda is happy to have been murdered.

But to Americans in 1892, her insistence on loving and wishing to marry and support a woman were, in and of themselves, clear signs of lunacy, and there was no shortage of physicians willing to corroborate that assumption. Still, in their efforts to create an airtight case, Gantt and Wright scoured Eastern Tennessee in search of the most prominent and influential physicians for supporting testimony. The prosecution had far less luck finding doctors to refute the plea, while the newspapers, sensing readers wanted some medical context, readily printed any theory that called itself scientific.

The first "prominent physician" quoted in a newspaper—or at least, the first one who made it to press—diagnosed Alice with erotomania, defining it, inaccurately, as "unnatural affection between two persons of the same sex." Other doctors, also unnamed, would assert erotomania was a "malady of the mind" that could easily "lead on to murder."[26]

Whether or not the unnamed doctors' quotes were fabricated by over-zealous newsmen, their alleged interpretations of erotomania were as legally convenient as they were medically creative. For more than two centuries before Alice murdered Freda, erotomania had described "forms of insanity where there was an intensely morbid desire to a person of the opposite sex, without sexual passion."[27]

While the Mitchell case would eventually produce new meanings, Gantt and Wright would not rely on the diagnosis of erotomania. In fact, the lawyers would avoid any argument that contained even a hint of the erotic, and most certainly any that acknowledged actual sex acts. Sex between two women was not entertained, even as a theoretical proposition.

The defense and prosecution, as well as most newspapers, tacitly agreed on this point: There would be no public discussion of anything even faintly sexual. Three years later, the English press would similarly cover the libel case Oscar Wilde lodged against the Marques of Queensberry, who left the writer a calling card inscribed, "For Oscar Wilde, posing somdomite *[sic]*." Wilde's sexual preference was never explicitly identified, but simply suggested through vague euphemisms, which included the very words the press seized upon and frequently applied to Alice—"unnatural," "immoral," and "indecent."[28]

That should not suggest the papers were unwilling to test the waters, even granting that Alice and Freda had experienced some "gratification of the perverted mental passion." The defense, however, was always quick to push back against these claims, insisting Alice and Freda's love was "purely . . . mental."[29]

WHO WAS ALICE MITCHELL? Why did she kill Freda Ward? Was she a masculine murderess? A pervert? A fast and jealous young woman? Or was she insane, like her mother?

Just as the Mitchells insisted that the defense argue for Alice's insanity, the Wards pushed the prosecution to maintain the opposite. "She was no more crazy than I am," asserted Ada's husband, William Volkmar, an "old Memphis boy" who had hosted Alice in his home.[30] Alice said "I don't care if I'm hung," Jo Ward recalled, insisting the murder was premeditated, and carried out in cold blood. Neither quoted the writer Mark Twain, but they would have found agreement in his essay, "A New Crime—Legislation Needed." Two years before Alice was born, Twain bemoaned the rise of the insanity plea, and how it allowed for otherwise unremarkable behavior to be recast as proof of an unsound mind.

Of late years it does not seem possible for a man to so conduct himself, before killing another man, as not to be manifestly insane. If he talks about the stars, he is insane. If he appears nervous and uneasy an hour before the killing, he is insane. If he weeps over a great grief, his friends shake their heads, and fear that he is "not right." If, an hour after the murder, he seems ill at ease, preoccupied and excited, he is unquestionably insane.

But it was the prosecution's case—and not the defense's plea—that newspapers characterized as inconsistent and unconvincing. Attorney General Peters called Alice "fast," citing jealousy over a man as a possible motive, but also claimed she was indifferent to men. At the very least, he argued that she was ill-tempered and vindictive, but certainly not insane.[31]

By questioning Alice's moral character, Peters challenged readers' cherished notions of the Mitchell family's respectability, and few outside the Ward family were interested in that perspective. The *Appeal Avalanche* soon reported that "the preponderance of public opinion is in favor of the theory that Alice Mitchell is insane."

Months before the lunacy inquisition would officially commence, the defense could claim public opinion as its first victory. Mass media played an influential role in regulating the boundaries of American modernity, and such a high-profile domestic tale on public display provided a means to do so. The defense offered editors a message they wanted to propagate: Alice was a well-to-do white woman from a pious family who was neither bad nor fast, and did not deserve to be in jail among base miscreants of every race and class. The public most certainly refused to see her hanged, with her fine family looking on.

Of course, the papers could not uniformly align themselves with the defense. Debate was a useful strategy when it came to selling copies; it was in the newspapers' interest to see that all positions were argued for vociferously. In Memphis, the *Appeal Avalanche* supported the case for insanity in lockstep with Gantt and Wright, while the *Commercial* often challenged them. If Alice had indeed loved Freda, the paper contended, she should be judged as a man would be, had he committed a crime of passion. She was legally responsible, they argued, "because she cowardly ran away. Had she been wholly irresponsible and insane, she might have acted differently after drawing the razor across Miss Ward's throat."[32] The *Appeal Avalanche* countered that the ability to function in daily life was irrelevant, as was any talk of treating a woman like a man, maintaining that Alice was "the slave of a passion not normal and almost incomprehensible to well-balanced people."[33] On that point, the *Commercial* almost always retreated.

Before Alice even entered the courtroom, newspapers across the country had latched on to every detail, real or imagined, of what they considered a particularly lurid murder. But national fascination with the case was about far more than the death of a seventeen-year-old girl, or a desire for entertainment and spectacle. Same-sex love, passing as a man, and alternate domesticities challenged everything Americans understood, and were desperately holding on to, in the late nineteenth century. During the next six months, this domestic drama would put issues of morality, individual liberty, and mental health front and center, forcing people to have a stance.

But first, Lillie Johnson would have to be arrested, and Freda Ward laid to rest.

CHAPTER EIGHT

MAIDEN PURITY

WHILE SOME REPORTERS waited outside the jail, others sought answers from the families themselves. They visited the Mitchell residence, where knocks on the door went unanswered. A few intrepid reporters managed to talk their way inside Lillie Johnson's home on Vance Street. Out of respect for her father, J. M. Johnson, local journalists promised they would leave—right after they had a quick look at Lillie, just long enough to describe her as "prostrated with grief" in the next print editions.

The Ward family lived up the river, but reporters would not find them in Golddust. Jo had sent word home with officers on the *Ora Lee*—the very steamer she and Freda were supposed to take home that day—instructing the Wards and Volkmars to board the next boat bound for Memphis. It is unclear whether or not, upon arrival, they knew that their youngest had died, or thought Freda had been injured, but would survive. They may have gone to the widow Kimbrough's house first, where they would return later that night as mourners taking refuge, but either way, someone directed them to Stanley & Hintons. The undertakers had already begun sealing the long, deep wounds on Freda's face and neck with wax.

It was reported that Thomas Ward was "pitiable on beholding the body of his dead daughter and fears are entertained for his mind."[34] It is highly unlikely that any reporter was allowed inside the room that held Freda's body, let alone present at the unveiling. But they were crowded outside, and some of them may have seen Thomas's face on the way out of Stanley & Hintons. In the first of many more instances of hypocrisy, reporters criticized citizens who waited beside them, displaying an "almost ghoulish" desire to see Freda's "mutilated face"—a sight they themselves seemed desperate to record.[35]

After a doctor had stitched Jo Ward's wounds closed, she joined the rest of her family at the undertakers, but the day she watched her sister

266 Whites
REGISTER OF DEATHS
1892

DATE.		NAME.	AGE. Years	Mo's.	Days	NATIVITY.
45545 January	20	Binkle Estella B.	3	1		Tenn
45546	"	Landdma Santa	72			Italy
45547	21	Hannon Budget	81			Ind
45548	"	Savage [illegible]	28			
45549	22	[illegible]				Tenn
45550	"	Croner Lea	3			
45551	23	McCollough Mary	67			Va
45552	"	[illegible]	32	3	2	Ky
45553	24	Peck J. C.	23			Ala
45554	"	O'Neil Wm	66			Ind
45555	"	[illegible]				Tenn
45556	"	Bennett Geo. [illegible]	4	5	2	Ala
45557	25	Frederica Ward	17			Tenn
45558	"	Quinlan Jas.	36			Ind
45559	26	Stabler Jas. Jr.		8		Tenn
45560	"	Taylor Martha L.	70			
45561	27	Humphries J. W.	43			Ind
45562	28	Willms Jas. [illegible]	50			N.Y.
45563	29	[illegible] Micheal		1?		Tenn
45563½	30	[illegible]	42			America
45564	"	Stewart Chas P.	43			Va
45564A	"	Hill C. [illegible]	81	9		Ind
45565	31	Daily Mary L.	66			

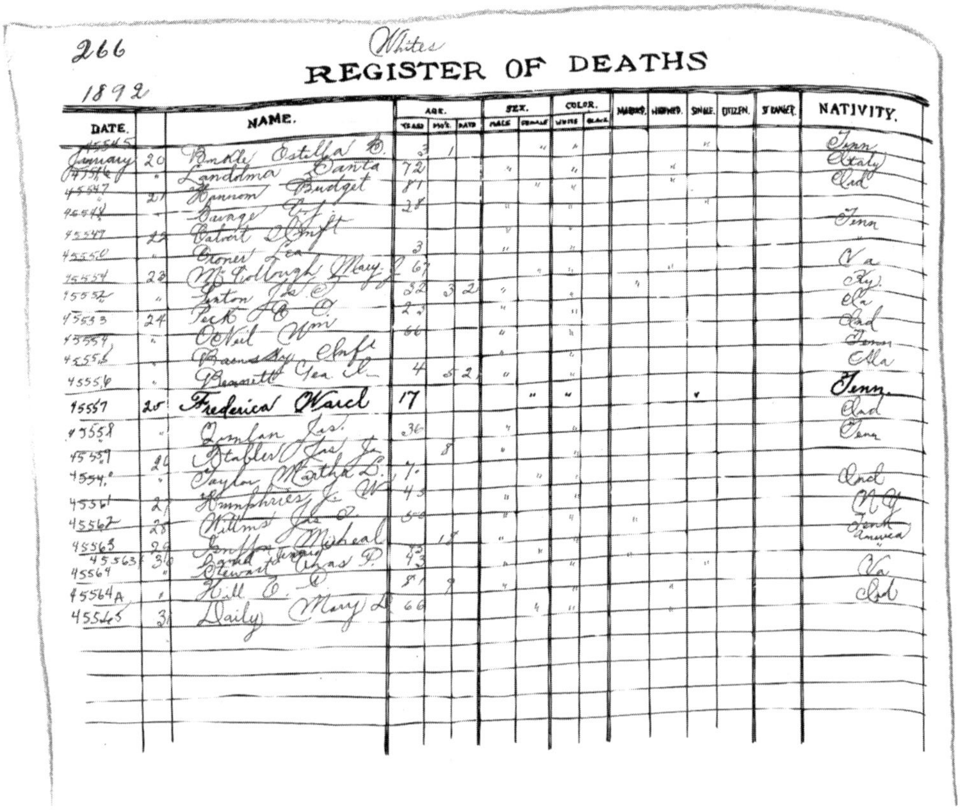

murdered was hardly over. The coroner insisted there be an inquest, and so Jo told her story once again, from the very beginning, going all the way back to Miss Higbee's. It was Jo who placed Lillie, the girl with whom she had once been chumming, at the scene of the crime.

By ten o'clock the next morning, Lillie was arrested at her home, escorted past the throngs of spectators outside the jail, and placed in a cell with Alice. According to newspaper accounts, J. M. Johnson accompanied her to the jail, but unlike George Mitchell, he remained there long after she was booked, lingering as close to his daughter as he was permitted, for days on end. Lillie was of a sensitive disposition, and her father remained nearby to offer whatever comfort he could. Reporters, however, had their own take on his extended stay: "He is fearful that Alice will do to his daughter some bodily harm and this fear is shared by all of his family."[36]

The papers would later criticize Lillie for offering no objection to sharing a cell with Alice, ignoring the fact that there were only two private cells in the whole jail. Alice and Lillie occupied one, and the other cell held attorney H. Clay King, charged with murdering another lawyer for sleeping with his wife—but his crime of passion was of little interest.[37]

With the single exception of Freda's funeral a few days later, the largest gathering of all occurred outside of the grand jury proceeding in downtown Memphis. As usual, a large, boisterous crowd gathered without the slightest hope of admittance; and, as usual, reporters denounced the public for showing interest in the very frenzy their newspapers were helping to fuel.

The press expressed particular vitriol toward African Americans. They were certainly allowed to be there, but in the 1890s, their role as spectator while a well-to-do white woman met her downfall presented a challenge—however slight—to the South's strict racial hierarchy. To diminish the power of their presence and reassert white superiority, the newspapers strained to characterize African American interest in Alice's case as more sordid than that of white courthouse voyeurs. To hear the press tell it, black

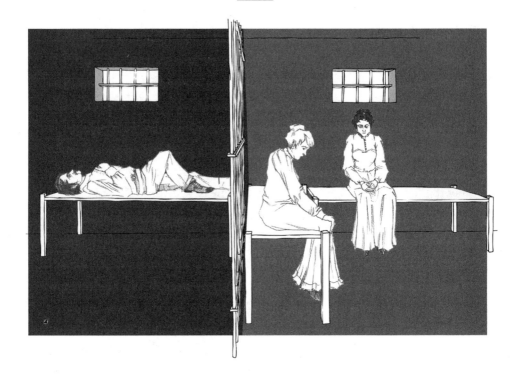

Memphians had only shown up because "their favorite weapon was used."[38]

The grand jury proceeding was closed to the public—and the records have been lost to time—but the outcome was soon known to all: Alice was indicted for murder. This was no surprise, but the fact that she did not bear the charge alone was; Lillie was indicted as well. She was generally regarded as an innocent bystander, a naïve friend in the wrong place at the wrong time, with one powerful voice of dissent: The attorney general argued that Lillie knew Alice intended to kill Freda, and did nothing to prevent it. Under Tennessee law, the burden of proof fell on the defendant, not the prosecution. In order to be released, Lillie would have to prove she had no prior knowledge of the murder. Her lawyer filed a writ of habeas corpus, but it would not be heard for weeks; Lillie's imprisonment had just begun.

In the few days since the murder, the legal stage for the case had only grown, and the plot had only thickened. Due to the local and national

Tuesday January 26th 1892

on this the 26th day of January 1892
T. J. Backhas
Foreman of the Grand Jury
Amanda Pen. Prosecutor
A True Bill
T. J. Backhus, Foreman of the Grand Jury

State of Tennessee,
vs   } Bench Warrant for Murder
Allie Mitchell

State of Tennessee,
vs   } Bench Warrant for Murder
Lillie Johnson
It is ordered by the Court that the Clerk of
this Court issue a Mittimus to the Jailer
of Shelby County Commanding him to secure
hold & detain in the County Jail of Shelby County
the said Allie Mitchell & Lillie Johnson until
further order from this Court or until they be
delivered by due process of law
Whereupon Court adjourned to 8½ oclock
tomorrow Morning
Julius J DuBose
Judge

attention the Mitchell case was receiving—and the needs of his own ego—Judge Julius DuBose ordered that the courtroom be expanded.

FREDA'S FUNERAL BEGAN AT THREE O'CLOCK—the same hour when, just three days earlier, Alice had spotted her leaving the widow Kimbrough's house. The memorial service was held at Grace Episcopal, the church where Alice and Freda had planned to wed, and was led by Dr. George Patterson, the reverend they had hoped would marry them.

Freda had been a cherished member of Grace Episcopal, and was "in general request whenever a church entertainment was given, having a decided turn for amateur theatricals."[39] On Sundays, she sang with the church choir, many of whom would perform somber hymns at her memorial. And she had attended Sunday school there, too, socializing with the young men who would now serve as her pallbearers.

But on that Thursday afternoon, the lurid circumstances of Freda's death meant that the pews held more than just family, members of the church and community, sympathetic friends, and acquaintances. The church was filled to capacity, and it was difficult to tell mourner and voyeur apart in the vestibule where her casket was displayed a half-hour before the service began.

The *Public Ledger* showed great restraint, avoiding descriptions of Freda's face in favor of just one comment about her body, which was "almost hidden from view in a profusion of white roses, emblematic of the maiden purity of the dead."[40] It was a brief, but significant editorial remark meant to reassure the public: One of their promising daughters had indeed lived her life honorably. Her pure, lifeless body could be covered in white roses because it was untainted by perverse longings, her life cut tragically short before she was able to achieve her potential as wife and mother.

The *Appeal Avalanche* was far less brief, complimenting the work of Stanley & Hintons as an unsubtle excuse to indulge in the grotesque.

The face wore a look of peace very different from the expression of despair that marked it before the skillful hands of the undertaker had closed the eyes and mouth and hidden the ghastly wounds through which the life blood ebbed away. The gash on her throat was entirely concealed, and the wounds on her check, chin and mouth were hardly discernible.[41]

Hundreds of spectators milled around outside, and accounts of their behavior varied, as always. Some of the newspapers praised the crowd for their respectful behavior: Eyes averted, hats in hand, and tones hushed. But other accounts described a rowdier scene, with gawkers so eager for a closer look that they tore the pickets off the church fence. All of the papers agreed that the overflow gathered outside of the church filled the adjacent yard to capacity, and the rest huddled outside of the houses that lined the block—including Lillie Johnson's home. As the mourning procession moved on to nearby Elmwood Cemetery, many more joined the crowd. They watched from afar as Freda's casket was lowered into the ground and covered with flowers, the grief-stricken Wards and Volkmars standing nearby. After the reverend spoke for the last time, members of the choir once again struck up hymns.

In the sweet by and by, they sang, *we shall meet on that beautiful shore.*

CHAPTER NINE

DELICATE HANDS, HORRIBLE DEED

ALICE MITCHELL WAS EXPECTED to make the briefest of appearances before Judge DuBose on February 1, 1892, but the Shelby County Courtroom was nonetheless bursting with bodies. Seats were quickly filled, and those who were left standing leaned against the interior walls, while others hoping to eventually wedge their way inside crowded the doorway. And though they had absolutely no chance of hearing anything of worth, and would likely get but a fleeting glimpse of the murderess as she passed by, the late arrivals lined the hallways and stairwells, and some even huddled outside, their breath visible in the cool, still air.

They all knew how Alice would answer the only question asked of her that day. They also knew that no evidence related to the crime would be seen, and that there was no chance of getting a sample of the most coveted of documents: the love letters that were being tightly guarded by both the prosecution and defense.

But this court date had little to do with facts, or even with the plea itself. This was the first real public performance, Act I, Scene I of a drama that would unfold for months in the theater of the courtroom.

It had been exactly one week since the murder, and even though the story was plastered across most national newspapers every single day, the information had grown stale. This was not for lack of effort. The influx of out-of-town journalists from big urban dailies crowded the local inns and boarding houses where they took meals and slept but a few hours. They spent the rest of their time racing around town, attempting to drum up whatever news they could, but there had been so little to work with. The public had yet to see all the actors in this production—the Mitchells and the Wards and the Johnsons, the defense and prosecution—gathered together in one room. All who were present in court that first day in February intended to make the most out of the mere minutes Alice would stand before Judge Julius DuBose. Having repeatedly quoted statements that Alice had supposedly made, the public would finally, albeit briefly, hear her voice.

Of course, there was always the hope she would put her alleged insanity on full display. Ideally, Alice would launch into a florid and picturesque manic episode, but spectators and journalists would settle for a glint of the eye, the slightest glimmer of madness. The opposing camp wished for any visual proof that she was a cold, vile, but completely sane killer.

The audience must have been disappointed, then, with Alice's brief appearance in the courtroom. Gantt and Wright fielded most of the questions while she sat beside them in silence, her face shrouded by a thick, black veil. Some interpreted this as an act of mourning, while others nodded in approval at the modesty of the Southern lady. Either way, the moment she lifted her veil and formally entered a plea of "present insanity," Alice became a public figure, in the flesh.[42]

The *Commercial*, the Memphis-based newspaper most critical of the insanity plea, thought that Alice had "an expressionless face, with low forehead, eyes together, and blotches that robs [sic] her of any pretense to a

Commercial

Appeal Avalanche

fair complexion."[43] They quoted a "well known priest" who deemed Alice "strong but not masculine," although her head had given him pause. This priest was quite sure, despite having only inspected her from afar, that her veiled head indeed contained a "disordered" mind.[44]

The *Appeal Avalanche*, sympathetic to the defense, painted a very different picture. Whereas the *Commercial* described her face (low forehead, close eyes, blotchy skin) in a way that was meant to make her seem unattractive, the *Appeal Avalanche* definitively concluded "Alice Mitchell is quite a pretty one." In its estimation, she was not "expressionless," but rather respectful and demure, her "large blue-grey eyes looked out quite complacently towards the judge." While the *Commercial* source characterized Alice as "strong," the *Appeal Avalanche* found its own unnamed witness to exclaim, "What delicate hands to commit such a horrible deed!" In a further effort to portray Alice as a non-menacing young lady from a respectable family, the newspaper spent some time detailing her distinctly feminine dress, from head to toe, including "a tan and brown checked ulster with a short cape . . . black Oxford shoes with little heels."[45]

Alice was not the only young woman submitting a plea that day. She was accompanied by Lillie Johnson, whose decision to join Alice for a buggy ride just one week earlier could now lead her to the gallows. Lillie pled not guilty, but the press hardly seemed surprised. Belief in her innocence was almost universal—with the notable exception of the attorney general. Peters's insistence that Lillie remain in a jail cell with an admitted murderess, one who many believed to be insane and perverted, was viewed as yet another strike against the prosecution's handling of the case.

But for the sake of news copy, Lillie proved to be a valuable courtroom counterpoint to Alice. Just as Freda had been described as far more girlish, Lillie displayed the kind of fragile grace that perfectly suited Victorian conceptions of femininity: "[Miss Mitchell] stood as rigid as a statue . . . Miss Johnson would have sunk to the floor but for the support of her father's arm."

THE MITCHELLS, WARDS, AND JOHNSONS were not exempt from such intense scrutiny. The public often rendered its judgments along gender lines that ignored, or even erased, the distinction between the defense and prosecution.

In this story, the fathers were stalwart characters, valiant protectors of women who faltered without their guidance, and flourished at their behest. Even when men from the Mitchell, Ward, or Johnson families were driven to rare displays of emotion—breaking societal expectations of the stouthearted, gallant Southern man—they still received positive reviews. The men, after all, had not failed to perform their duties. The home was the haven fathers returned to after a day out in the world doing men's work, while women remained near the hearth. It was the guardian women, the mothers and older sisters, whose responsibilities began and ended in the domestic sphere; they were the ones who had fallen short. After the failure of their wives and daughters, the men had no choice but to hold strong as lionhearted fathers and husbands, shoring up their families during exceptionally trying times.

These men—George Mitchell, Thomas Ward, and J.M. Johnson—were presented as not merely blameless, but almost victims themselves, sympathetically called the "three sorrowing fathers."[46]

George Mitchell—father of the confessed murderess, husband to a purportedly unstable wife—was a retired businessman described as being "well suited to leisure." Before the trial interrupted his life of ease and recreation, Uncle George had a reputation for being a gamesman with a particular fondness for guns. From the moment he turned Alice over to the warden's care, George had captured the sympathy of the nation, and most certainly of his fellow Memphians. They saw him as a fine man who was doing all he could, having hired the best lawyers around—which may have also meant the most expensive. George was risking the entire Mitchell family's financial future to care for his youngest child, tainted as she was through the matrilineal line. The Mitchells were all beleaguered, but it was only George who was described as having worn the stress on his face. He had aged so rapidly, reporters observed, that he now appeared but a "poor old man."

Thomas Ward, whose wife and, as of a week prior, youngest daughter, had predeceased him—both dead well before their time—was regarded with the kind of respect naturally granted to the bereaved. Even so, the papers could not resist painting his grief in shades of gender. Upon hearing of Freda's death, it was reported that Thomas was "almost unmanned" by the loss.[47] But like all displays of emotion by men, the moment passed dec-

orously, as it must, and it was his background of consummate manly efforts that defined his public persona: his attempts to better his family's fortune in Golddust, to leave behind his job as a machinist at the Memphis Fertilizing Company and try his luck as a merchant and planter, all while making sure his daughters were tended to by his eldest, were regularly lauded.

Even Lillie's father, J.M. Johnson, whose name was rarely mentioned in the press, was given his due. Reporters spoke of him with admiration and reverence for the way in which he doted on his daughter, and consistently praised him for the nights he spent at the jail, keeping an eye on his Lillie. Much like the rest of the historical actors involved in the case, few personal details were offered about J.M. Johnson, including his profession; it was never named by the press, though a Memphis city directory listed his occupation as painter.[48]

In newspaper articles, however, the maternal figures were treated with little regard, or worse: they were often depicted as teetering on the edge of insanity. Though their supposed instability was sometimes explained by the stress of the murder, more often than not, the women were portrayed as being plagued by long-term "hysterical" tendencies. Which is to say, the murder itself was tacitly blamed on the folly and feminine ineptitude of the women who should have been responsible.

It did not help that Isabella Mitchell, Alice's mother, rarely made public appearances. Newspapers noted that her only outings seemed to be long visits downtown with Alice, where she would ignore the press vying for her attention as she entered and exited the jail.[49] Despite her reticence to engage, Isabella was spoken of often, her mental history was discussed in newspapers and in the courtroom; the defense would painstakingly review her hospitalizations in order to establish hereditary history, a requirement of the "present insanity" plea.

Freda was murdered a decade after her mother died, at which point her eldest sister, Ada Volkmar, became her surrogate mother. Although Ada was credited as the only person from either family to uncover the elopement in time to stop it, she was not commended for her foresight or her decisive action. No one seemed very interested in the steps she took to intervene, or the maternal authority she wielded over Freda. With just one disastrous exception—the last note she sent before supposedly quitting Memphis—Freda had cut off all contact with Alice, just as Ada had commanded. And

it was Ada who informed Isabella of Alice and Freda's plans, and likewise implored her to impose a similarly tough stance. But the press rewarded Ada's diligence by vaguely describing her as "not well," a condition that was ironically the effect of the murder far more than, as the newspapers insinuated, an underlying cause of it. She rarely appeared in court.

Mrs. Johnson, Lillie's mother, was yet another woman said to suffer from "nervous prostration," and was thus confined to her room. Similarly, Mrs. Kimbrough, still playing host to the Wards, was said to have been experiencing heart trouble from all of the excitement the case had brought into her life. In the usual custom, the women's first names were not mentioned.

In other words, the matrons were portrayed as incapacitated or silent or, most commonly, both. The young women, particularly Jo Ward, were held in high esteem as long as they demonstrated the kind vulnerability expected of women in the Victorian era.[50] And of course, the prettier, the better.

REPORTERS WERE NO DOUBT GLAD TO SEE Judge Julius DuBose, a notoriously bombastic character in Memphis, sitting on the bench. He was both intolerant and despotic, a misogynist and avowed bigot whose colorful interludes would earn their fair share of space in the dailies.[51]

The son of a wealthy planter, Judge DuBose was an early leader in the Tennessee Ku Klux Klan, and former editor of the *Public Ledger*.[52, 53] He was elected to the criminal court in 1886, but his heavy-handed tactics earned him plenty of enemies. Impeachment proceedings against him would begin in 1893, a year after Alice was arrested for Freda's murder. In fact, it would be Luke Wright, one of Alice's own attorneys, who would prosecute Judge DuBose before the state senate on an impressive tally of thirty-four counts. He would be impeached and convicted twice—for failing to recognize a writ of habeas corpus and overstepping his authority—but his position was eventually restored.

MEMBERS OF THE JURY had yet to be selected, but the press was not deterred from spirited conjecture. No juror who called himself a Southern gentleman, declared the *Commercial*, would indict a young, white lady from a good family. Even though the evidence was substantial and Alice's guilt "indisputable," the *Commercial* bemoaned the possibility of any judgment against this poor young woman of good standing. The tone of its coverage seemed to criticize—but was actually applauding, in advance—the Memphians who would eventually determine the fate of the nineteen-year-old woman. If there was one thing the nation should know about the men of Shelby County, the *Commercial* assured readers, it was that "their chivalry exceeds their sense of justice."[54]

The jurors' identities were still unknown, but their skin color and gender were not: The jury box was guaranteed to be stocked with white men. The Civil Rights Act of 1875 may have stated that "no citizen possessing all other qualifications which are or may be prescribed by law shall be disqualified for service as grand or petit juror in any court in the United States, or of any State, on account of race, color, or previous condition of servitude," but by 1883, inconsistent state rulings would culminate in a landmark Supreme Court verdict. The Justices overturned the law eight-to-one, ensuring people of color were denied the right to participate in the judicial sphere.[55]

What would happen if women *could* serve as jurors? The *Commercial* hypothesized that an all-female jury—by which they surely meant white women—would be free of the chivalrous regard expected of their male counterparts, and would thus find Alice Mitchell guilty. But, of course, this was a theoretical scenario; in 1892, women were barred from the polls, and even after the right to vote was finally won in 1920, states continued to deny them the opportunity to serve on juries. The very presence of women in the Shelby County courtroom was a peculiarity of the case, and while it was considered a challenging dose of modernity, an anomaly tolerated because the unusual saga was understood to have moral implications.[56] Gender rules, it was thought, could be relaxed for a hearing that would ultimately reinforce them.

THERE WERE CONCERNED but vastly outnumbered Memphians who implored the papers to pay less attention to the case, hoping it would allow for a speedier trial.

> It is most devoutly to be wished that the trial of Alice Mitchell and Lillie Johnson may take place at a very early date, and the case removed from public consideration. Its prolongation would be deplorable. It is one of those cases which appeals strongly to morbid sentimentality and which tends unduly to excite disease of weak minds.[57]

But the trial was of the utmost importance to the nation for reasons far greater than entertainment—though it was certainly an added attraction. All the major mass media publications flocked to Memphis for the first time because the Mitchell case was not just about two young women, same-sex love, murder, or even lunacy—it was about American modernity.

In the 1890s, the predominant national identity of whiteness—one that had been disrupted by the Civil War, Reconstruction, and an influx of Chinese and Mexican immigrants—was a narrative more uncertain than ever before.[58] Whiteness was an inherently unstable ideology, constantly threatened by economic and political upheaval, and now Alice provided yet another perceived menace to the existing narrative: a gendered threat to white men's authority, challenging their power across the spectrum—particularly in the domestic sphere. This was a battle for their own homes.

The kind of violence Alice had displayed with her father's razor was a "masculine" act as much as it was a privilege of white men. If anyone else was seizing it for themselves—as the nascent suffrage movement, demands for broader political enfranchisement, calls for fair wages and greater opportunities suggested—the traditional power base of white America was in peril. And women were just the beginning. Soon all races and classes would follow. For many white men, the bloody developments in Memphis illustrated the dangers they collectively faced. It served as a dire call to claim what belonged to them, and to which they were duty bound, by natural and civil laws, to protect.

CHAPTER TEN

ATTENDANCE EVEN
GREATER THAN OPENING DAY

LILLIE HAD BEEN FRIENDS with Alice for years, but in the months before the murder, it was as if she hardly knew her. When Freda cut off contact with Alice, Jo had done the same with Lillie, but her exile came with no explanation. Without any knowledge of Alice and Freda's foiled elopement, the sudden severing of friendship with the Wards, especially with Jo, had been a great loss for Lillie—and a baffling one. She was confused and hurt, but her close-knit family offered solace, as did other friends. At that point, Lillie was far more concerned about Alice, who seemed altogether changed.

But nothing in Alice's dark and brooding moods could have prepared Lillie for the events of that late afternoon in January. She had no idea that, while she lingered behind in the buggy, an old friend was being murdered at the hands of another.

"Oh! What have you done to her?" Lillie cried from the buggy as Alice barreled up the hill.

Alice climbed back into her seat and roughly steered the buggy away, ignoring Lillie's questions. She rode with only one hand on the reins, while the other she shoved deep into her dress pocket, desperately fishing around for the razor, and, in the process, bloodying Freda's last letter to her. Alice feared she had dropped it during the melee—and she wasn't done with it.

Had everything gone as planned, Alice would have first cut Freda, and then herself, so that the two lovers could bleed out in each other's arms in one final—and eternal—embrace. But Jo and the growing crowd had interfered, and in the ensuing struggle, Alice had lost track of the razor. Only days later, when her sisters searched the buggy, did the murder weapon reappear. By that time, she and Lillie would be together once again, this time as cellmates in jail.

Having safely maneuvered the buggy onto Court Street after the murder, Alice finally answered Lillie's question.

"I have cut Freda's throat," she said.

"No, you haven't—have you?" Lillie cried in disbelief.

"Yes, I have," she said.

Alice had given up on the razor, and countered with her own alarming question. "What is the quickest way I can kill myself?"

"Don't do it while you are here with me," Lillie pleaded, still piecing together what was happening. "Go home and tell your mother what you have done."

"Is there much blood on my face?" Alice asked, to which Lillie answered yes, as she held her young nephew close. Alice was covered in blood, a steady stream dripping down her face and onto her coatdress.

"Take my handkerchief out of my pocket," Alice ordered, "and wipe it off." But as Lillie moved a finely woven cloth toward her friend's face, a new realization came to Alice.

"Oh, no," she said now. "It's Freda's blood. Leave it there. I love her so."[59]

"LADIES TO THE RIGHT, AND GENTS TO THE LEFT," bellowed Judge DuBose.[60] It was as if he were directing revelers in a dance hall, and not throngs of voyeurs at the habeas corpus hearing of a teenaged girl. The question of whether Lillie Johnson would be escorted back to Alice Mitchell's jail cell or returned to her family was to be determined, and nobody wanted to miss a minute of the show.

It did not matter that no verdict would be handed down on that day in late February, 1892, or that an appearance by Alice was in no way guaranteed. Lillie may have been a minor character in the same-sex love murder, but it was still the hottest ticket in town. In the days before every American household had a radio and television, entertainment options were scarce;

just like a theater troupe passing through town, a sensational trial offered a rare and brief spectacle. If the day's show starred Lillie, then people happily turned their attention to her.

It had been a month since the grand jury indicted Alice and Lillie, and weeks since the arraignment, but the public's interest had not waned in the least. Every moment of this case was unfolding like a serial drama, and the eager audience wanted to see the story progress.

Records of the grand jury proceedings have been lost, and its deliberations were closed to the public, but we know at least one witness testified that Lillie had been present during the murder—and had done nothing to prevent it. When Alice herself confessed to the authorities, she revealed that it was Lillie who had directed her home, to tell her mother of the murder, rather than advising her to proceed immediately to the police station and surrender. Under Tennessee law, that was enough evidence to charge Lillie with "aiding and abetting" Alice Mitchell in the murder of Freda Ward. It was on the basis of that testimony that she was taken into custody and held without bail.

Lillie's attorneys argued that the grand jury lacked sufficient evidence to warrant their client's arrest, but in order to prove it, they would have to call their own witnesses to the stand. It would be the first time that testimony was heard in an open courtroom, and *that* was what the public had come for.

But the show had been delayed until construction work on the courthouse was completed. Well aware that the case had become a national obsession, and that the local economy was getting a boost from the influx of visitors in town, Judge DuBose's unorthodox request to expand the Criminal Court in Shelby County was granted—even though it took almost a full month to do so. Every few days, the court date was pushed back once again by the construction project. But Judge DuBose was enjoying the frenzy and attention, making full use of the time. His name appeared in the newspapers every single day; family, friends, colleagues, acquaintances, and assorted others called on him at the courthouse and at his home at nearly every hour in pursuit of information. He had no hesitation about continually postponing the trial date to accommodate all corners—especially members of the press.

Knowing that the press was in control of the day-to-day public narrative of the trial, Judge DuBose made sure journalists had the best seats in the house. He ordered a special section of box seats for the press, a move that immediately set off squabbles among the reporters over which paper deserved the best spot. But even with the expanded space and the reserved seating, demand quickly overwhelmed the room. Reporters who managed to secure box seats were quick to mock those who scrambled around them.

The clamoring crowds gathered at the courthouse and the general public's frantic curiosity in the trial were becoming the case's main storylines. "Another Day of Thrilling Interest in the Criminal Court, The Attendance Was Even Greater Than on Opening Day, Opera Glasses Leveled on the Cowering Defendant Witness," exclaimed the *Memphis Appeal Avalanche*.

It did not take long for one newspaper to distinguish itself from the pack. It was not the *Appeal Avalanche*, the *Commercial*, nor the big out-of-towners, like the *New York Times* or the *San Francisco Chronicle*. Judge DuBose's former employer, the *Memphis Public Ledger*, was by far the most popular news outlet. It was available at the conclusion of each eventful day in court, however inconclusive, with exhaustive commentary on every detail of the unfolding case, keeping readers coming back for more.

According to the *Public Ledger*, Judge DuBose's courtroom had quickly become the most democratic public place in all of Memphis. By the time President Abraham Lincoln issued the Emancipation Proclamation in 1863, Tennessee had abolished slavery and returned to the Union fold, but Jim Crow laws helped maintain the South's rigid, deeply entrenched racial hierarchy. These segregation laws mandated that African Americans were kept "separate and equal"—meaning separate and unequal. They ensured systematic economic, educational, and social disadvantages well after the Civil Rights Act of 1964 and the Voting Rights Act of 1965 were passed.[61] But in this rare instance—the theater that was Judge DuBose's courtroom—people from across class, race, and gender lines shared a space.[62] They sat side-by-side as they would in almost no other setting in Memphis.

Staid Matrons and their young daughters sat check by jowl with women of doubtful character and women whose lack of all character was blazoned on their faces as plain as a pikestaff. There were white and black, mulattoes, quadroons, octoroons and a sprinkling of the genus whose class has never been distinctly defined—all eager to see two of their sex in peril of their lives, and hoping, perhaps, to hear something excitingly naughty."[63]

Female spectators, who DuBose separated from the male spectators, featured prominently in print. The press, who were almost all white and male, never failed to describe the women's craning necks, distracting bonnet plumes, and artificial flowers—all with a palpable degree of disdain.

"The best place for ladies to sit during the trial is about four feet from the hearthstone," the *Avalanche Appeal* complained.

Judge DuBose himself took the lead on that front, constantly reminding women, lest they forget, that their continued attendance in the courtroom was at his discretion, and he could easily have them removed. But behind these displays of white male authority was a distinct anxiety *about* white male authority; the press and the judge made a point of asserting their power precisely because they were unnerved by the prospect of women watching courtroom proceedings and drawing their own conclusions. Alternate domesticities, such as two women coupling and sharing a home—and even the general notion of females expressing passion—were considered inap-

propriate for the "fairer sex," especially for ladies of the higher classes. It was no coincidence that female witnesses went to great lengths to dress conservatively, donning capes and jackets over their dresses, and often covering their faces with heavy veils removed only upon request. And at that point, they further exaggerated modest affectations, bowing their heads until they were again told otherwise.

It was one thing to allow women inside the courtroom—seated apart from men, of course—but no individual woman's place was secure. Judge DuBose took a particular dislike to one Sarah Davis, whom the press quickly nicknamed "Buckskin Lou." Her greatest transgression seemed to be in occupying a seat between two white women even though she looked "like a Mexican," and wore a dress with a bright print. Judge DuBose criticized her each day of Lillie's habeas corpus hearing, until finally, he expelled her. Like everyone else in the courtroom, Sarah Davis had worked hard to secure a seat, showing up early and claiming a spot amid the tussle, and she was not about to give it up without a fight. After the court adjourned, she waited for the judge, and a heated scene quickly ensued, much to the delight of reporters standing nearby.

> "Go away, woman; I don't want to talk to you," Dubose said.
> "I won't go away. I know my rights. I won't be ordered out."
> "Mr. Officer," said the judge, "take this woman to jail."[64]

Judge DuBose took every opportunity to exercise his authority over the court's eager spectators, which only deepened the tensions in and around the Criminal Court, and heightened the public's already anxious anticipation to see defendants and witnesses in person.

And then, it finally happened: Alice Mitchell and Lillie Johnson entered the courtroom, leaning heavily on the strong arms of their escorts, George Mitchell and J.M. Johnson, respectively. Either their older female relatives were absent, or the women had become so skilled in the art of self-effacement that not a single newsman noted their presence.

CHAPTER ELEVEN

QUITE A FLIRT

MUCH TO THE PUBLIC'S DISAPPOINTMENT, Alice did not stay long. Her lawyers, still eager to control her story, would have preferred that she never enter the courthouse at all that day. Gantt and Wright almost certainly forbade Lillie's attorney, a junior at their own firm, to call Alice to testify at his client's habeas corpus hearing. Alice's lawyers hoped to make it to the final verdict without ever having their client utter a word in public.

Unfortunately for them, Alice's presence in court that day was necessary for the defense's motion. The Ward family had entrusted Freda's collection of love letters to the state, and it had become a real point of contention. Gantt and Wright had already sent several requests to the attorney general's office, but they refused to furnish the letters until the trial. But Alice's lawyers were desperate to see them now, not when their client's lunacy inquisition finally arrived. At best, a surprise would leave them scrambling, and at worst, it would determine whether or not their client would hang.

As the *New York Times* predicted, prosecutor George Peters countered the motion by making his own request "for an order requiring the defense to permit him to inspect certain letters in their possession, which he would very much like to get a peep at."[65] But Peters was not particularly interested in seeing the defense's letters. He was, in fact, far more concerned by the level of interest the defense had in his letters, which he kept locked away in the attorney general's office.

Peters was a respected prosecutor with personal experience when it came to crimes of passion: His own father, Dr. George Peters, Sr., had murdered Confederate major Earl Van Dorn for supposedly having an affair with his wife. But nothing in Peters's background, or the ample evidence he believed proved Alice was sane and should be tried for murder, seemed to help him with this case. He was overextended in his current post, and far too reliant on young, relatively inexperienced assistants.[66] The battle for public opinion had already exposed his office's weaknesses, and so Peters, eager to gain back some advantage, strenuously argued against the defense's request for the letters. And for once, he was met with some success. Judge DuBose was uncharacteristically swift in granting him the right to keep all letters sealed until Alice's lunacy inquisition.

After their motion was denied, throngs of disappointed journalists and curious observers watched the entire Mitchell family, including Alice, of course, file out of the newly expanded courtroom. They had come no closer to seeing Freda's letters, nor had the public seen or heard anything noteworthy from the murderess herself. And it would be months before they would see her again, not until winter and spring had passed, and summer was in full bloom.

COMPARED TO THE MITCHELLS, the Johnsons were of modest means. But they had the good fortune to live near "one of the most promising young men at the bar," as the *Commercial* put it. The Johnsons had become well-acquainted with their young neighbor, Malcolm Rice Patterson, and at just the right time: Had they attempted to procure his services just a few years later, he surely would have been too busy to take on their case.[67] Patterson was a Southern Democrat steadily climbing the political ranks; by 1907, he would be the Governor of Tennessee.

Patterson came from an old Memphis family of great prestige. His father, Colonel Josiah Patterson, had been a formidable Confederate commander during the Civil War, and went on to be a representative in the Tennessee State legislature, a candidate for governor, and a member of U.S. Congress. He had joined his father's law firm, Gantt and Patterson, and it behooved him to work closely with Gantt himself on such a high profile case.

He was tasked with convincing Judge DuBose that Lillie had made the innocent mistake of getting into Alice's buggy on the wrong day. Lillie had no prior knowledge of Alice's intention to murder Freda, and she was unaware of what was happening even as the crime was being committed. Lillie's entire focus that afternoon, Patterson would argue, was not on revenge against Freda or loyalty toward Alice, but most immediately on her young nephew, who was in her care. Lillie was a family-oriented young woman who belonged back at home with her loved ones, not in jail with a murderess who everyone knew—because Patterson's own law firm repeatedly told them—was insane.

Newspapers tended to portray Lillie as a vulnerable, deferential young woman. There was much talk of her public displays of "nervous prostration." She was understood to fare poorly under even the slightest emotional strain, and the case was believed to have greatly exacerbated her condition, leaving her visibly pale, exhausted, and physically weak. Her father or brother was usually by her side when she stood or walked, and as close as possible when she sat in court or was returned to her cell, should she be suddenly overcome by these most unfortunate circumstances. It was suggested that she suffered from "female hysteria," a catchall diagnosis for women who appeared faint and nervous; symptoms included insomnia, sexual desire, and shortness of breath. This affliction—which is no longer recognized by physicians—was used to describe almost any undesirable emotion. In court, it would work in Lillie's favor.

And she would need every advantage she could get. The grand jury had, after all, indicted Lillie. Even the press, who doubted her involvement in the murder, remained unsure as to whether or not she was a good, pious girl in the wrong place at the wrong time, or a "fast," perverse girl who might as well remain in jail with Alice, lest she start consorting with the chaste daughters of Memphis in her friend's absence.

In the courtroom, the public learned about Lillie's less than virtuous behavior. The rumors that she flirted with streetcar conductors were not going away, nor was this immodest behavior the end of the story.[68] Like Alice, Freda, Jo, and presumably many of the students at Miss Higbee's, Lillie had answered ads placed by young men in the matrimonial papers. During an era when courting options were limited, there were publications, like San Francisco's *Matrimonial News*—which had originally catered to lonely men who ventured West during the Gold Rush—that were entirely dedicated to putting single people into direct, and often unsupervised, contact. Although the young ladies of Memphis had access to such periodicals, they were more likely to use the local paper's classified sections, where bachelors placed advertisements.

Under the pseudonym Jessie Rita James, Lillie exchanged flirtatious letters with, as the *New York Times* called them, "callow youths." The letters were themselves relatively harmless, but the press and prosecution called her propriety into question. Why, they asked, had she kept her identity a secret? Why had she kept the correspondence hidden? Knowing that her mother would certainly disapprove, Lillie had taken care in concealing her actions, relying on her brother's downtown office to funnel correspondence. No one was suggesting that Lillie had met these men in person, but the matter was

clear. She consistently engaged in an unseemly activity—which could have easily crossed into the realm of true scandal—and she had demonstrated a capacity for subterfuge. Lillie had taken dangerous risks and lied unabashedly. Were those not the traits of a person who acted as an accessory to murder?

Even if Lillie was not *legally* culpable for the bloody events of January 25, in the eyes of the nation, Alice was as a cautionary tale. Freda's murder illustrated that any young woman's misdeeds, no matter how slight, could quickly turn into the worst and most vicious form of immorality.

Lillie's continued loyalty to Alice only encouraged such speculation. Much was made of the cell Alice and Lillie shared, but no one seemed to care whether or not there was another option. There were only two private rooms in the jail, and the other one was occupied by a man who was also charged with murder; she could have been grouped together in a communal cell with women of ill repute, who were being held on charges like larceny, or far worse. Still, they wondered, why would an innocent woman agree to share a confined space with an admitted murderess, especially one with "unnatural" proclivities?[69] If Lillie was engaged in this type of behavior, even under such public scrutiny, then what, the paper insinuated, would she do when nobody was watching?

Her relationship with Alice, one that long predated the murder, was clearly at the heart of the matter. Alice longed for a life outside of what the domestic sphere offered her, and could not be controlled by family or social norms. She had openly rebelled against the rules of society—and Lillie had been just mere feet away during most of it.

The most compelling evidence against Lillie was not her proximity to the crime scene, but rather her assistance on a number of Alice's prior spy missions, including an expedition just a week before the murder. Alice had asked Lillie to join her in confirming her suspicion that Freda was lying about her departure date, and she had obliged, accompanying Alice onboard a Golddust-bound steamer. This suggested, the prosecution argued, that Lillie knew of Alice's machinations, and was indeed an active participant.

But, of course, Lillie knew very little about Alice and Freda's relationship. Yes, she had witnessed the aftermath, when the Wards suddenly and inexplicably severed ties with both Alice and Lillie, but by the time she discovered the case, it was already front page news. When she boarded that steamer, Lillie was working under the mistaken assumption that they were simply seeking answers about the sudden rupture. In a letter to Jo—which went unanswered—she sought the very information that everyone, the Wards and Alice alike, had been keeping from her.

Memphis, Tenn, Jan 5, 1892

Dear Joe - I know you are angry with me and I won't asked you to be a friend of mine, but please tell me why you are angry. I want to know, so that when people asked me I know what to tell them. Tell me what you are angry with me for and I will tell them what you tell me to say.

Lillie

During her habeas corpus hearing, Attorney General Peters presented the letter as evidence and argued that it established Lillie's motive: She was angry and hurt, he reasoned, and that was why she helped Alice, or knowingly neglected to stop her from committing her ghastly deed.

The letter threw Lillie's attorney for a loop, but Patterson was quick on his feet, and used the evidence to draw a distinction between Lillie's confusion and Alice's focus. Lillie's behavior might appear untoward, he allowed, but even by contrast, it was hardly as odious and vile as Alice's actions. They were all gathered in the newly expanded courtroom, after all, because of a singular lunatic named Alice Mitchell. But in order to make his case, Patterson would have to call Jo Ward, the letter's recipient and Lillie's old chumming partner, to the witness stand.

JO WAS QUESTIONED TWICE by both the defense and the prosecution. They struggled to bend her testimony to fit their versions of the story, all the while trying to remain sufficiently reverent of a family in mourning. They had to be especially careful when it came to Jo, a traumatized witness to her own sister's gruesome murder. Jo was stricken with grief, and she dressed the part, taking the stand in a heavy, head-to-toe black mourning dress. The public sympathized with her loss, and further pitied the Ward family for having to rely on public representation, while the Mitchell family could hire powerful lawyers.

It also helped that Jo was considered quite pretty and, even under such trying circumstances, demure and charming, always exhibiting the utmost propriety. Even after she was ordered, in the gentlest of terms, to lift her veil, she hesitated, much to the approval of the courtroom. And when her handsome face was finally revealed, she kept her head bowed, and avoided eye contact with male spectators.

Jo conceded that her old friend Lillie had always possessed a "gentle nature"—even after Ada had abruptly ordered an end to their close relationship. Jo also confirmed that, on the day her sister was murdered, she had not seen Lillie anywhere near the scene of the crime; not then, nor earlier, when she, Freda, and their friend Christina Purnell had quit Mrs. Kimbrough's for the riverboat landing.

Jo's account of the murder was exactly what the courtroom had been waiting to hear—and luckily for the defense, it was a story in which Lillie made no appearance.

> What first drew my attention to the cutting was Miss Purnell's screaming, and as she screamed I turned around . . . Miss Mitchell was right at my sister then, and was nearly cutting her. She was cutting at her, and I struck her with the umbrella. She turned to me and said: "I'm going to do just exactly what I wanted to do, and I don't care if I do get hung."
>
> After she said that, she jumped up and flew up the levee,

running very fast . . . She had blood on her face and on her hands, with a great deal on one side.[70]

Having established his client's absence from the scene of the murder, Patterson moved on to background questions. The packed crowd in the courtroom sat in rapt silence, preparing for what they knew would come next: the highly anticipated account of the same-sex love affair between Alice and Freda.

Without a moment's hesitation, Jo, followed by the prosecution, objected to Patterson's line of questioning. It was distracting. It was irrelevant. It was indecent. But Judge DuBose disagreed, and permitted Patterson to continue.

"Is it not a fact that your sister forbade your having anything to do with, or writing to Miss Johnson and Miss Mitchell, because Alice Mitchell and your sister were engaged to be married, and your sister was about to elope with her, and had gotten on the boat for that purpose?"

"That was one reason," Jo answered.

"Was that not the *controlling reason?*"

Judge DuBose again ignored the prosecution's protests, but cautioned Patterson—the man who would one day be governor—to remember there were women with delicate sensibilities in the audience, and they were unaccustomed to hearing talk of such profane and worldly subjects. Though the judge disagreed with their very presence, they were in his courtroom, which made him their chivalrous protector.

Patterson accepted the warning, and proceeded as gently as possible, with Alice and Freda's plan to meet in Memphis.

"And there marry? Well, now, in that arrangement to marry, Miss Ward, who was to be the man? Miss Mitchell?"

"Yes, sir."

"[Freda] intended to take the boat, did she not, and to come to Memphis, and then they intended to go to St. Louis?"

"Yes, sir."

"And your sister was to be the wife, was she, and they were to arrange it in that way?"

"Yes, sir."

"And was not Miss Mitchell to be called Alvin J. Ward after they married?"

"Yes, sir."

"Your sister was to be called Mrs. Alvin J. Ward?"

"Yes, sir."

"That was all made up and understood, and planned, and your sister discovered it all, and after making that discovery she forbade your further correspondence with them?"

"Yes, sir."[71]

Judge DuBose had allowed Patterson's probe, and thus granted the prosecution permission to reexamine Jo, who had certainly noticed the defense's approach. What was it about Lillie, Peters asked, that had so bothered Ada? What could have been so terrible about Lillie that Ada forbade Jo from ever seeing her again?

"It was because she visited the union depot quite often, and she flirted a great deal. She flirted with men . . . . When she was visiting us last summer, my sister also forbade her waving at the boats and the men," Jo explained. "She was just considered quite a flirt."[72]

At that, Lillie nearly fainted.

The accusation that she had shamelessly flouted accepted gender norms, the revelation that her immodest behavior was the reason she was banned from talking to her best friend, and the fact that all of this—her disgrace—was announced in a crowded public courtroom and, within hours, in newspapers across the country, was too much for Lillie to bear. Aiding and abetting a murder was one thing, but shameless flirting was something else entirely.

It was just one o'clock, but Judge DuBose adjourned the hearing. Lillie had become so distressed by the first day's proceedings that he considered it unwise to continue. She would remain unsettled well into the night, until the sheriff deemed it necessary to summon a physician to the jail.

FAIR LILLIE

DAY TWO WOULD BE EVEN WORSE. It was Lillie's turn to testify on her own behalf. She appeared weary and frail. Halfway
through a description of her five-year friendship with Alice, she started
sobbing, setting off a ripple effect through the sympathetic courtroom.[73]
More than one newspaper ran her story on the front page with the headline
"Fair Lillie."

But soon enough, questions about her friendship with Alice receded
into the background, and the attorneys turned to the central issue: Freda's
murder. Lillie recounted the more mundane events of that day in late January when she, too, had been grateful for the break in inclement weather.
She remembered having been out and about, including a morning visit to
the blacksmith with Alice, where her friend, unbeknownst to her, had very
specific plans to have the horses shod in time for the steamer's departure.
When they parted ways for lunch, Lillie assumed it would be the last she
saw of Alice on that winter day, and she would devote the rest of it to
her family.

And yet, when Lillie and her sister were walking back from a quick shopping trip downtown just a few hours later, they ran into Alice, who seemed keen on taking the buggy out.

Since finishing at Miss Higbee's, afternoon rides were often the most exciting part of their day, but the outings had never been terribly consistent. This was an important point for the defense, and Patterson labored over it, lest there be any suspicion that Lillie knew what her old friend really had in mind for that afternoon. When Alice eventually materialized at the Johnson family's front door around two o'clock, Lillie was caring for her young nephew, and thought the ride suitable for him as well.

If Lillie had known that they were headed into a murder scene, Patterson repeatedly asked, would she have brought him along?

With two members of the Johnson family in tow, Alice drove past Mrs. Kimbrough's house where, indeed, Freda was spotted; she then proceeded toward Madison Street, as Lillie wished to stop by her brother's work for a brief visit. Lillie admitted she had noticed the Ward sisters and Christina Purnell walking on the street, but since Jo was no longer speaking to her, she had specifically asked Alice not steer the buggy in their direction.

Alice held the reins, but assured her that they were only going to the post office, and Lillie had no reason to doubt her. In light of the scandal made in court of her correspondence with young men, it no doubt pained Lillie to sit on the stand and admit she thought nothing of stopping at the post office; the business of sending and receiving mail was an exciting part of their lives.

"Oh, Lillie," she recalled Alice saying. "Fred winked at me. I am going to take one more look at Fred and say good-bye!"

At the post office, Lillie preferred to stay with the horses. She was still sitting in the buggy when she saw Alice running up the hill. Between the obscured view and caring for her nephew, she had no idea what had just transpired, nor any reason to suspect foul play. To her knowledge, Alice had never threatened Freda, or said anything to indicate she had a capacity for violence. Lillie knew that Alice was far more hurt by their estrangement from the Wards, but assumed Alice's experience with Freda mirrored her own with Jo. The dissolution of their friendship had been an unfortunate and confusing loss, but not a totally devastating one.

It was the blood that opened her eyes. Alice was covered in it. Lillie knew something had gone terribly wrong, but Alice ignored her questions until the horses were in motion again, trotting down Court Street. Having had little worldly experience, and coming from a particularly tight-knit family, Lillie could think of only one piece of advice for Alice in the heat of the moment: Go home and tell your mother. It was a sad irony that this suggestion was the very thing that was used to incriminate Lillie, since it could clearly be traced back to her upbringing as a proper young woman, instructed to obey her mother's dictates.

The courtroom could have handled more from Lillie, but she was unable to offer it. Her physician, Dr. Z.B. Henning, and her family priest, Father Hale, had already testified to her "delicate health." Her father and brother spoke to "a sick headache" that had long plagued her. Lillie's condition had forced her to withdraw from a covenant school near their former home in Indiana, and then again from Miss Higbee's in Memphis.

Judge DuBose once again softened upon seeing her fragile state, and excused her from further testimony. It was clear that Lillie was delicate, some-one to protect from the conditions of jail and the kind of women it housed—especially Alice Mitchell. The audience, though disappointed, approved of his paternalistic compassion as much as Lillie's display of weakness.

PETERS WAS EVENTUALLY ALLOWED to cross-examine Lillie, which he did very carefully so as not to draw the ire of those who sympathized

with the young woman. While Lillie's obedience was understood as a desirable trait in the Victorian era, Peters wanted to portray it as feckless and shifty. To link her behavior to the ugly traits of a criminal, he needed only ask Lillie why she accompanied Alice home after the slaying.

"[Alice] asked me to stay, and I would do anything for her," Lillie replied.[74]

The attorney general savored her answer. Lillie would do *anything* for Alice. Even after Alice admitted to murdering their friend, Lillie would still do *anything* Alice asked of her.

After that, Peters moved away from the murder entirely. His focus shifted to the letters Lillie sent under the name Jessie Rita James, reminding the judge that she was not only "fast," but untrustworthy. In those letters, she had lied about her identity, and she had also lied to her mother by concealing them. Would it not be logical, then, to assume that she was also lying about her involvement in the murder? Lillie, Peters argued, had a motive (anger at the Wards for ending their friendship), a secondary motive (she would do *anything* for Alice), and a critical skill (she was a known liar) that was essential to any murder plot. She was, Peters argued, a moral threat to other respectable girls—just as Alice had been to Freda.

By the time Peters was done, Lillie seemed wholly unsteady on her feet.[75]

THE AUDIENCE AT LILLIE'S habeas corpus hearing had noticeably dwindled after the first day, but Alice's absence was not the only reason. Lillie's fits of "female hysteria" were convincing enough that even the *Commercial,* the newspaper typically suspicious of the defense, concluded that "few of those who heard the words of this unfortunate girl and the testimony of others yesterday morning, believe that she is guilty of murder as an accessory."[76] The sharp decline in attendance suggested that the public agreed.

No doubt disappointed that his spectators believed this part of the show could be missed—after he had expanded his own courtroom to accommodate them—Judge DuBose injected a dose of drama back into the hearing. He took two full days to deliberate over Lillie's fate, which elicited the intended response; the public took notice, wildly speculating as to the cause of the delay. Was there a surprise element that had given the judge pause? Did Lillie belong in jail? Was she actually a threat to the daughters of Memphis?

By the time Judge Dubose read his statement, every seat in the court-room was once again filled.

"The proof is evident that the defendant aided and abetted in the commission of the crime, a crime that [is] most atrocious and malignant ever perpetrated by woman," he read, ever so carefully, from a prepared statement.[77] Despite the dramatic, seemingly ominous beginning, Judge DuBose acknowledged Lillie's fragile condition and awarded her temporary freedom, should the Johnson family meet bail, set at $10,000.

The Johnsons were not wealthy, but the monies were somehow arranged, and Lillie was freed to everyone's momentary delight. It was the *Public Ledger,* and not the *Commercial,* that cast a shadow of doubt on the ruling, observing that Lillie "moved with a sprightly step for one so ill."[78]

To the public, Lillie's habeas corpus hearing was only a rehearsal for the real production, but it would be summer before Alice's inquisition of lunacy brought all of the actors back into the theater. And for that event, Judge DuBose's manufactured drama would prove unnecessary.

CHAPTER THIRTEEN

THE OLD THREAD-BARE LIE

BEFORE LILLIE WAS ARRESTED, Alice had spent just one night—the night of the murder—alone in jail. But now that Lillie was back at home with her family, Alice was all alone again, with an extremely short list of permittable visitors, and a relatively long wait before her case would be heard in court.

If Alice kept any records of the six months she spent in jail, they have been lost, but it seems unlikely that she would ever again commit her feelings to the page. Her letters from the last few years, especially those precious ones she and Freda had exchanged, were now being bandied about by men as power plays. They wanted to define who she was, to appropriate her personal story—her love—by controlling documents that contained her most intimate concerns. And the worst humiliation was yet to come. It was only a matter of time until those love letters were presented in court, and then reprinted in newspapers across the nation. If Alice had written letters or kept a journal while she was behind bars, she probably disposed of it herself, rather than relying on someone else. At that point, who could

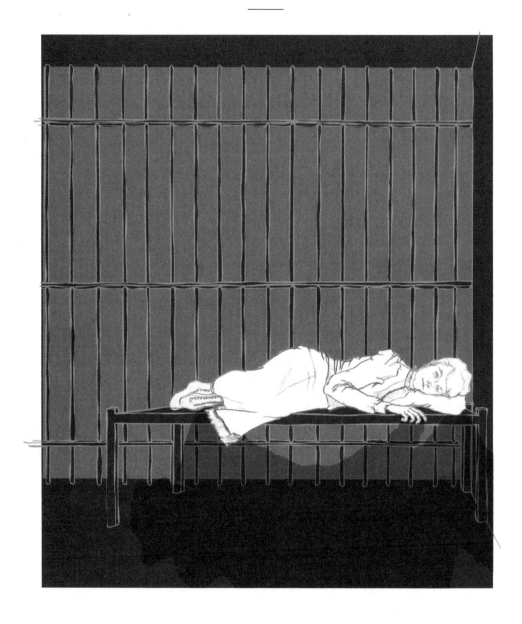

she trust? She had asked Freda, her love, to destroy her letters—and that request had obviously been ignored.

Like so much about Alice, we will never know exactly what it was like for her to be alone in jail during those long months before the lunacy inquisition. At best, we can surmise that the many weeks and months were plagued by loneliness and gloom and monotony.[79] At worst, life in jail was downright frightening.

IN THE EARLY HOURS OF MARCH 9, 1892, Alice may have been asleep in her cell, but it was unlikely she slept through the night. A mob of angry white men descended on the jail between two and three in the morning, demanding that three African American men be released into their custody. Had Alice not committed murder, she would have never resided in a cell near the men they were after, and had the jail they all occupied not been in turn-of-the-century Memphis, those men may not have been incarcerated at all. But she was in jail, and that meant she might have seen what justice looked like from the other side.

Calvin McDowell, Thomas Moss, and Henry Stewart were joint operators of the People's Grocery Company, a cooperative market in "the Curve," Memphis's densely populated African American neighborhood. The Curve already had a grocery store, owned and operated by W.H. Barrett, a white man who resented the competition. It was one of a series of clashes over the nature of free market competition reverberating throughout Memphis. The city's white population had become incensed at the increasingly improved economic status of, and increasing competition posed by, African Americans. In this case, tensions reached a head after store hours, when Barrett entered through the front door of the People's Grocery, and his white friends through the back.

The People's Grocery had been expecting this, and had sought legal counsel in advance. The Curve was a mile beyond city limits, and there was no police protection, thus the three men were advised to arms themselves—but with extreme caution. In the heat the moment, however, three of the intruders were wounded. They wore plain clothes for afterhours trespassing, but during the day, it turned out they donned the uniforms of deputies. Once McDowell, Moss, and Stewart realized this, they threw down their firearms and offered themselves up for arrest. The injured aggressors were taken to the doctor, and the ones who had initiated the violence but emerged unscathed were let go. Dozens of African Americans were arrested and taken to jail. Bail was denied, as was communication with the outside world.

It is hard to imagine that a posse of angry white men, out for blood, was met with much resistance at the jail. This was a group whose members Alice, and likely most white Memphians, would have recognized. Some were neighbors, and others were likely community and business leaders.

It was rumored that Judge Julius DuBose—who presided over all of the cases in the jail— was among the white mob in those early morning hours. If he was not part of the gang, he was certainly sympathetic to their cause. His personal history was typical of white men who felt threatened by social and economic changes in the post–Civil War South. He had been raised by a planter who benefitted from slavery. His family suffered financially after their slaves were emancipated and they were finally required to pay wages to those who stayed on as staff. The judge was a founding member of the Tennessee Ku Klux Klan, not simply out of bigotry but, it seems, as a way to protect the material interests of his family and community.

Thomas Moss, Calvin McDowell, and Henry Stewart were taken to an open field just outside of the city limits. Their bodies were later found, disfigured by shotgun and buckshot wounds. McDowell's eyes had been gouged out, and his fingers reduced to bloody stubs.

The *Appeal Avalanche* celebrated the lynching for being "one of the most orderly of its kind ever conducted."[80] No white men were ever arrested for participating in the horrific killings.

The next day, the sheriff led a hundred men to the Curve with strict instructions to "shoot down any Negro who appears to be making trouble."[81]

To give the whites an even greater advantage, the arms and ammunition of the Tennessee Rifles, the African American guard, were confiscated. The money drawer of the People's Grocery was emptied by those tasked with patrolling the Curve, who also helped themselves to various goods, no doubt celebrating with the wine and cigars they pilfered. Barrett bought whatever stock was leftover—at one eighth of its cost—and added it to his own store's offerings. The message was received, and the People's Grocery did not survive long after the lynching.

Alice may have heard the lynching that night. She may have known those being lynched. It is almost guaranteed that she knew at least some of the men who carried out the lynching. Regardless, they all lived in the same city, and travelled on the same roads. Alice probably passed Thomas Moss during Freda's stay at the widow Kimbrough's home. He was one of the oldest letter carriers in Memphis, and had continued to deliver mail while the nascent People's Grocery worked on becoming a sustainable business. His route included the office of the *Free Speech*, the African American press on Hernando Street.

News of the lynching quickly reached Ida B. Wells, a twenty-nine-year-old editor and writer whom Thomas Moss had befriended. She was enraged by the brutal murders—and unsettled by them. There had been a sharp increase in lynchings in Memphis, with the violence usually justified as retribution, an appropriate form of vigilante justice after allegations of rape by an African American man.[82] Wells, born a slave in Holly Springs, Mississippi, was well acquainted with this rationale. But the People's Grocery lynching lacked any accusation of sexual assault. The retaliation was mostly economic in motivation, clearly meant to reinforce white preeminence in Memphis.

Two months after the lynching, Wells began to write a series of groundbreaking, provocative editorials rejecting "the old thread-bare lie that Negro men assault white women." She warned men of the South who terrorized those around her with impunity: Their continued violence would inevitably force a realization that "will be very damaging to the moral reputation of their women."[83] If white women engaged in sexual relations with African American men, it likely occurred because they instigated it.

An African American paper daring to publish the news that white men were lying, that they were using the virtue of their women as an excuse for violence, would itself have been a major affront in the 1890s. The suggestion that, in the rare instances when sex between black men and white women did occur, it was the white women who had likely *invited* the transgression absolutely incensed white Memphians. The outrage expressed by local papers—the same ones covering Alice's case with the utmost reverence for white fathers and a paternalistic view of women—declared it an unbearable degradation that should be handled immediately, and without restraint.[84]

The *Public Ledger's* only nighttime competition, the *Memphis Evening Scimitar*, assumed Wells was a man, and that the community should make an example out of him.

Patience under such circumstances is not a virtue. If the negroes themselves do not apply the remedy without delay it will be the duty of those
whom he has attacked to tie the wretch who utters these calumnies to a
stake at the intersection of Main and Madison Sts., brand him in the forehead with a hot iron and perform upon him a surgical operation with a pair
of tailor' shears.[85]

They did not brand or carry out any other form of violence on Wells,
but it was not for lack of trying. A white mob, one that may have again
included Judge DuBose, destroyed the *Free Speech* offices on Hernando
Street. By that time, they had realized that Wells was a woman, but their
much lauded sense of chivalry did not extend to African American women.
Wells was out of town during the violence, but her absence did not go
unnoticed. If she returned, the vigilantes promised a lynching. She ultimately left Memphis for New York, where she would become one of the
most well known and respected political activists in America.

IN ADDITION TO ALICE MITCHELL, Ida B. Wells was the only other
woman in 1892 Memphis whose story was circulated around the country.
Both women undermined, challenged, and disregarded white male authority in very different ways—and the reactions they garnered, and the treatment they received, had far more to do with their respective races than
the transgression itself. White men threatened to kill Wells for what she
wrote, whereas no one wanted to see Alice, who actually committed murder, hanged for her crime.[86]

Wells, Mitchell, and the operators of People's Grocery lived concurrent
lives in the same city, but they occupied distinct social, physical, and economic
spaces within it. That separation has certainly influenced our collective memory, but their stories shaped crucial moments in twentieth century America.[87]

In the 1890s, the United States was cementing its national identity, and it was predicated upon maintaining the white home on a national level. Same-sex love and African American men and women were cogent threats to the rigid hierarchy of race and gender, and the reactions on a local level from the judge, jail, sheriff, and newspapers speak to the national construction of American modernity.[88]

PART III

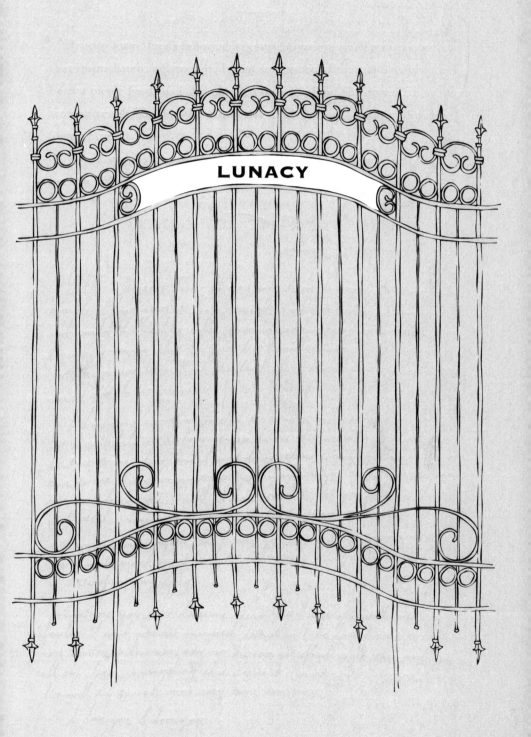

LUNACY

THE HYPOTHETICAL CASE

BY THE TIME ALICE MITCHELL'S lunacy inquisition began on July 18, 1892, the defense was ready. Gantt and Wright had spent the months following Lillie's habeas corpus hearing much as they had spent the days following the murder: crafting a message, finding support for it, and then skillfully releasing the information to the public.

They had allowed some access to Alice, but exclusively to the area's most prominent medical experts—all of whom could be counted on to offer a diagnosis of insanity.

The prosecution also attempted to solicit medical experts, but they could not find anyone willing to support the position that same-sex love did *not* equal insanity. The superintendent of the Western Hospital for the Insane in nearby Bolivar, Tennessee, declined to even meet with Alice, admitting he was convinced by what he read in the papers.[89]

And therein lay the brilliance of the present insanity plea: It explained what appeared to be inexplicable, and recast a murderess as the sympathetic victim of her own illness.

If the plea failed, however, it would only be a matter of time before Alice was sentenced to death. A murder trial would have to take place first, but given her confession, a guilty verdict was all but guaranteed.

In 1892, "present insanity" was not unlike our modern day understanding of "incompetent to stand trial." Alice's mental state at the time of the murder was a concern, but of far less importance than her current mental state. However, in order to establish "prior insane conduct," Alice's lifelong mental state, from birth up to the present, was relevant. The defense's case was laid out in "The Hypothetical Case."[90]

Much like the initial statement circulated by the defense, which read like an interview, the Hypothetical Case was a relatively short, narrative biography of Alice Mitchell. Her life, from birth to the present day, was reduced to just twelve pages.[91] It was a preview of the defense's legal strategy, incorporating both the testimony they would present in court, and the input of expert witnesses who would take the stand over the next ten days.

"Alice was a nervous, excitable child, and somewhat under size," it began, proceeding to illustrate how her traits, interests, and behaviors had intensified over her lifetime. In a strategic move, the defense leaked the psychiatric vignette to the press ahead of the inquisition. It appeared in newspapers read by the public and, most importantly, by the jury. The Hypothetical case provided a roadmap that led to one obvious conclusion: Alice was a victim of her body—just as Freda had been.

"The question is, whether the defendant has mental capacity sufficient to make a rational defense to the charge in the indictment," Judge DuBose told the jury.[92]

Though it was presented as a narrative, all the information contained in the document could be filed under a list of six major points integral to the plea: poor health, bizarre conduct, unfeminine behavior, masculine interests, improper attachments, and finally, the role of hereditary influence.

THE HYPOTHETICAL CASE

Alice was a nervous, excitable child, somewhat under size. As she grew she did not manifest interest in those childish amusements and toys that girls are fond of.

When only four or five years old she spent much time at a swing in the yard of the family in performing such feats upon it as skinning the cat, and hanging by an arm or leg. She was fond of climbing, and was expert at it.

She delighted in marbles and tops, in base ball and foot ball, and was a member of a children's base ball nine. She spent much time with her brother Frank, who was next youngest, playing marbles and spinning tops. She preferred him and his sports to her sisters. He practiced with her at target shooting with a small rifle, to her great delight. She excelled this brother at tops, marbles, and feats of activity.

She was fond of horses, and from early childhood would go among the mules of her father and be around them when being fed. About six or seven years ago her father purchased a horse. She found great satisfaction in feeding and currying him. She often rode him about the lot bareback, as a boy would. She was expert in harnessing him to the buggy, in looking after the harness, and mending it when anything was amiss. To the family she seemed a regular tomboy.

She was willful and whimsical. She disliked sewing and needlework. Her mother could not get her to do such work. She undertook to teach her crocheting, but could not. She was unequal in the manifestation of her affections. To most persons, even her relatives, she seemed distant and indifferent. She was wholly without that fondness for boys that girls usually manifest.

She had no intimates or child sweethearts among the boys, and when approaching womanhood, after she was grown, she had no beaux and took no pleasure in the society of young men. She was sometimes rude, and always indifferent to young men. She was regarded as mentally wrong by young men toward whom she had thus acted.

About the time her womanhood was established she was subject to very serious and protracted headaches. She had far more than the usual sickness at that period. She was subject to nervous spells, in which she would visibly tremble or shake. She is still at times subject to these attacks of extreme nervous excitement, but does not, now, and never did, wholly lose consciousness in them but upon one occasion.

In order to convince the jury that Alice was "presently insane," the state also required that the defense establish "hereditary influence." This was not a notion particular to Tennessee, as F.L. Sim, one of the doctors called in to assess Alice, explained in the *Memphis Medical Monthly*. In the nineteenth century, bodily pathology, or symptoms that began in the body and could therefore be inherited, were considered "the most common and potent of all causes of mental disturbances."

Fortunately for Gantt and Wright, Isabella Mitchell's history of congenital insanity was "proven beyond a doubt."[93] The Mitchell family's physician, Dr. Thomas Griswald Comstock, offered a convincing disposition, and brought a copy of her "certificate of confinement" as evidence.

Following the birth of Isabella's first child in 1857, George Mitchell grew concerned about his wife's displays of melancholia.[94] He called Dr. Comstock, who, after a month of house calls, confirmed Uncle George's suspicions. Isabella was diagnosed with "puerperal insanity," a derangement or

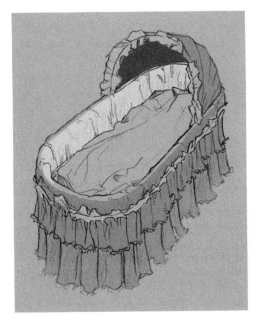

unstable state brought about by childbirth, and placed in a hospital. During her stay, she supposedly passed from melancholia to insanity to acute mania, and finally, to recovery. After two months of restraint, she was released, and eagerly returned home, excited to see her infant.

But in Isabella's absence—and possibly as a result of it—the infant died. She was not told of the death until she arrived home, and began searching for a baby who was no longer there. When she discovered the tragedy, Isabella was understandably shocked and overcome with grief—or, according to Dr. Comstock's testimony, "her mind became again unbalanced." Perhaps fearing that her husband would once again have her institutionalized, Isabella managed to resume her wifely duties in just a few days, though she still displayed the signs of melancholia that had first landed her in the asylum.[95]

Isabella gave birth to seven children during her lifetime, only four of which would survive to adulthood.[96] According to testimony, she "evinced more or less mental disturbance with each parturition, especially after the birth of Alice." This was a salient point in a nineteenth century courtroom, where psychiatrists understood the defendant's disease to be of the body. When Isabella had Alice, her final and most challenging pregnancy, they believed she had passed her insanity on to her daughter.

The symptoms associated with puerperal insanity were constantly shifting, but they all amounted to a condition that undermined true womanhood. The illness was broadly defined to include, at one end of the spectrum, women who denied their baby nourishment, or seemed to pose an actual danger to them. But it also included mothers who appeared disinterested in their offspring. Women who were gloomy, or apathetic to the needs of those around them, unkempt or seemingly overwhelmed, were also diagnosed with puerperal insanity—sometimes called "insanity of pregnancy," or "insanity of lactation." By World War I, the designation disappeared and was replaced with "postpartum depression."[97]

Dr. Comstock's treatment points to a problematic relationship between the predominately male physicians and their female patients. This kind of power dynamic was a privilege that extended widely to encompass all men at the time—hence George's influential role in both his wife and daughter's diagnoses. As Michel Foucault points out in his book *Madness and Civilization*, the physicians who sought to define reason also silenced "unreason," and this became a convenient way to regulate people, even whole classes of people, whom society labeled deviant.

The defense lawyers carefully crafted the Hypothetical Case in order to prepare the public for their courtroom performance, and to ensure that testimony stayed on message. They relied on family members and other witnesses who knew Alice to substantiate the claims and anecdotes during the first half of the lunacy inquisition, and for the expert witnesses to do the same during the second half.

And while Gantt and Wright did everything in their power to avoid it, Alice Mitchell would indeed take the stand.

VICARIOUS MENSTRUATION

" I DON'T CARE IF I'M HUNG," Alice screamed during the murder, but her family did. The Mitchells' testimony, which was unfailingly consist-ent with the defense's Hypothetical Case, would not only help Alice avoid certain death, it would ensure her speedy disappearance into an asylum.

If Alice was found presently insane, it would not void the murder charge, but it would indefinitely postpone it. She would be sent to the state lunatic asylum for "treatment." If physicians were pleased with her progress, they could reassess her, and determine her well enough to stand trial. Whether the case would be reopened or not would be up to the state, but it was unlikely to ever reach that point. Once Alice went into the asylum, she had very little hope of ever getting out. It was as good as a life sentence.[98]

With that goal in mind, George Mitchell was the first witness to be heard at his daughter's long awaited hearing. He was motivated on that summer morning, and delivered a moving performance on the stand. George spoke to the court with great emotion, sharing the history of his wife's puerperal insanity, and the way it seemed to intensify with each birth, just as Alice's own odd behavior had progressed each year. And yet, despite his most valiant efforts, he had failed to save his women from themselves. The saga was so painful to relive, it brought George to tears.

Isabella Mitchell, who bore him seven children, was not in the courtroom that day. She did not hear her husband, or the doctor who had committed her time after time, painstakingly review how Isabella's body had been poisoned by her own family, just as she had unwittingly poisoned her youngest daughter's body. The puerperal insanity had turned Alice into someone capable of perverse, unnatural love and, ultimately, murder. Isabella was noticeably absent throughout the hearings, but she could read all about her own insanity in a variety of newspapers—as could all of her friends and family, her church, and neighbors. Everyone was now familiar with her medical history, and its consequences.

IT WAS ONE THING TO SATISFY the hereditary component, but quite another to support the defense's claims that the murderess's body had displayed physical symptoms of insanity. Gantt and Wright called older sisters Mattie and Addie to the stand, and asked them about Alice's nosebleeds. Both sisters remembered that the bleeding had begun when Alice was twelve years old, or as the Hypothetical Case placed it, "around the time her womanhood was established."

Of course, Mattie and Addie were quick to point out that *they* had not suffered from nosebleeds—it was a condition unique to Alice. Whenever possible, the Mitchell family was sure to juxtapose their own normalcy with Alice's strangeness, an approach that served a dual purpose; the family maintained respectability while drawing attention to Alice's illness. For their own sake, it had to be clear that Mattie and Addie had escaped their mother's insanity.[99]

Alice's nosebleeds had not been diagnosed at the time. It was not until a certain Dr. Callender, one of the doctors who interviewed Alice in jail, offered his professional opinion, declaring it "vicarious menstruation."[100]

The Mitchells could offer far more examples of behavior that transgressed gender boundaries than evidence of bodily symptoms. They focused on Alice's preference for her brothers' physical activities, and indifference to her sisters' comparatively domestic pursuits. Mattie and Addie's dolls had never excited their youngest sister, but their brother Frank admitted Alice "could pump in a [baseball] swing" better than he could. Their half-brother, Robert, took the stand armed with the props of boyhood—baseballs, marbles, and other decidedly unfeminine evidence—taken from Alice's bedroom. His youngest sister had always favored her brothers and preferred to play with boys, Robert said with the authority of a man twenty-one years her elder.[101]

By the time Lillie confirmed that Alice had been on the baseball team at Miss Higbee's, as if it were a revelatory admission, Attorney General Peters had heard enough. He took issue with the defense's emphasis on sports, asserting that it had nothing to do with insanity, nor was it even rare. After all, Alice had not *started* the baseball team at Miss Higbee's. It existed before she enrolled, and when she joined, her name was added to a roster of other young women who enjoyed sports, but still acted in an otherwise non-homicidal manner.[102]

Still, Alice's preference for boys as playmates, not romantic interests, was a surprisingly persuasive argument in the courtroom. It suggested that she had not formed appropriate associations as a child, and subsequently developed aggressive behaviors alongside her male counterparts. Later in life, when it was time for her to experience romantic yearnings, Alice continued to mature as a boy would—by developing an interest in girls.

Despite the courtroom presence of Alice's friend, Lillie, whose material importance to the case was undeniable, experts agreed that Alice suffered from an inability to develop proper attachments. She was confused by her early proclivities, they said, and was unable to differentiate between female friendships and prospective suitors.

Lillie's brother, James Johnson, age twenty-one, shared a personal anecdote to illustrate Alice's unresponsiveness to men. He recalled the time he approached her, outstretched in a hammock with Lillie, and asked her to dance. Alice refused James—who, for all we know, smelled of garlic and told bad jokes—preferring to lay alongside his sister.

Addie confirmed that Alice showed no interest in the men who came to court her, and refused to receive their calls. She was capricious, the Mitchells added, and sometimes refused to speak with the family at all.

After that, the personal testimony given during the first five days of the hearing—by family, friends, and neighbors—became progressively vague. "I felt as if there was something wrong with her, but I couldn't say what it was," testified Mrs. Charles Mundinger, who attended the same church as the Mitchells. The family's butcher made a brief appearance, recounting the time he called Alice a tomboy. Her damning reaction? She did not balk, testified the butcher.[103]

HEREDITARY INFLUENCE, SOMATIC EVIDENCE, and a history of odd behavior all played a significant role in establishing Alice's supposed insanity, but the single most important factor—the one that dominated the Hypothetical Case—was Alice's relationship with Freda.

"The attachment seemed to be mutual, but was far stronger in Alice Mitchell than in Fred[a]," read the statement. The theory was supported by a variety of physical evidence, including the engagement ring bearing the engraving "From A. to F.," as well as what the public was most desperate to see: the love letters.

Having kept aloof from Alice during her darkest period, the Mitchells could barely speak to her obvious heartbreak—but Lucy Franklin could. The "Negress," as she was identified by the press, testified to Alice's anguish and despair, and how she suffered after the estrangement. Her behavior was consistent with what was known as "love sickness," a popular term used in nearly all articles on crimes of passion during the nineteenth century. It served as a kind of justification for any violence that might ensue after heartbreak. The prosecution repeatedly argued that it applied to the case, but the disconnect between Alice's same-sex love and the traditional model of love-sickness-turned-crime-of-passion (forsaken woman murders temptress over a man's love) rendered it irrelevant.[104]

Alice seemed to have trusted Lucy more than anyone else in the Mitchell home. She showed her the contents of the secret, locked box in the kitchen, and told Lucy dramatic stories about her devastating loss, and how it made her want to die. There was the laudanum incident, of course, when Alice had intentionally ingested the potentially lethal poison. But Lucy divulged another unsettling incident, in which Alice held the family's rifle to her own ear. In the excitement, she had accidentally let out a few shots, but remained unharmed.

Even though Lucy found the length and depth of Alice's torment worrisome, and did truly sympathize, she seemed to eventually regard it as self-indulgent. Lucy was a domestic worker in the segregated South. After a long day laboring for the Mitchells, she probably had just as much work, if not more, to do in her own home. The double shifts left her exhausted, and unable to lessen many of her family's immediate concerns, no matter how hard she worked. Tellingly, Lucy tried to comfort Alice by pointing out her privilege, recalling that she tried to explain that "there was no use to worry as she had plenty of money."[105]

The Mitchells also had difficulty describing Alice and Freda's relationship before the murder, and what little they did manage to say was heavily informed by the same sources everyone else had access to: the newspaper articles and the Hypothetical Case. The Mitchells' unique insight came from their visits to jail, and they all agreed that Alice appeared to be unremorseful, both of her love for Freda and the brutal murder itself. They claimed Alice spoke of Freda in the present tense, as if she were still alive.

Even the *Commercial* was becoming increasingly convinced of the insanity plea:

> Had she slain a man who had deceived or betrayed her, the idea of insanity may have never been presented, but she slew a girl for whom she entertained a passion such as exists ordinarily between members of the opposite sexes, and the peculiarity of the case at once gave color to the suspicion of insanity.[106]

Freda's family, however, remained unconvinced. They agreed that the idea of two women eloping was strange, but they had distinct memories of Alice's behavior in their home, and they saw no evidence of insanity. Alice should be held accountable for Freda's death, the Wards maintained. They wanted to see her tried for murder.

William Volkmar, who had waited, Winchester rifle in hand, for a man to claim his sister-in-law the night she planned to runaway, testified that Alice was sane. She had even displayed affection toward men in his presence. Jo Ward repeated this refrain, informing the court that Alice was a member of the Pleasant Hour Social Club, and had attended its dances with male escorts.

Alice had indeed gone to such dances, but her reasons for attending were never entirely clear. A romantic interest in men may have been the obvious impetus, but perhaps it was just easier to attend and socialize. She could satisfy expectations *and* keep a watchful eye on Freda, who also attended the dances. Furthermore, Alice's escort was one of convenience, a young

man a couple of years her junior. He was not a romantic interest, and it was clear that, outside of Freda, Alice had not shown romantic feelings for anyone else, male or female.

As Wright pointed out, Alice might have gone to the Pleasant Hour dance with a young man, but she went home with Freda. Most interested parties avoided any explicit mention of a sexual relationship between Alice and Freda, which put defense in a bind; They had to find a way of mentioning the unmentionable. The more deviant Alice's love for Freda, after all, the stronger the claim to insanity. And yet, the extreme deviance of same-sex love, the bizarreness of it, meant that it appeared to be unprecedented to most people's minds. How does one speak of the existence of that which does not exist? It was a rhetorical tightrope walk, as demonstrated in these two highly suggestive lines from the Hypothetical Case:

Time strengthened the intimacy between them. They became lovers in the sense of that relation between persons of different sexes.

And with that, the first half of the ten-day inquisition drew to a close. The defense was still in the lead, but it had been far more of a volleying match than they had expected, with Attorney General Peters's litigation skills proving to be a formidable challenge. The second half, however, would be decisive.

AN IMPOSSIBLE IDEA

DURING THE SECOND HALF of the inquisition, the defense called five medical experts to the stand, while Peters, unable to lure a single physician to support his case, had only his courtroom acumen to depend upon. The expert testimony would be highly influential, but Gantt and Wright were saving the best for last—though they did not yet know it. Alice Mitchell would take the stand.[107]

The doctors had received the Hypothetical Case in advance, despite the prosecution's attempts to render it inadmissible as hearsay. Judge DuBose allowed it, since each of the experts had personally interviewed Alice in jail, at least once, for no less than an hour.

All five prestigious physicians concurred with the Hypothetical Case, and did so with great authority. Dr. John Hill Callender, who had introduced the term "vicarious menstruation" to the court, was a sixty-year-old Nashville native and longtime medical superintendent of the Central Hospital for the Insane. He was also a professor at the University of Nashville and Vanderbilt University, where he earned a statewide reputation for his work with nervous diseases.[108] Dr. Frank L. Sim, a fifty-eight-year-old professor at the Memphis Hospital Medical College, was also held in great esteem, and from there, the other doctors' backgrounds were varied enough that the defense could claim they sought opinions far and wide—at least within the state of Tennessee. It did not matter that it was hard to differentiate between each expert's testimony. On the contrary, consistency only reinforced the impression that the opinions were objective, the result of rigorous scientific methods.[109]

Before they had even met Alice, the doctors agreed she had a hereditary disposition. In jail, they observed her to be of low intelligence, noted her supposedly vacant facial expression, and above all, documented a complete lack of remorse. One doctor, E. P. Sale, cited Alice's left-handedness and slightly asymmetrical features as further proof of her condition.

The expert witnesses primarily focused on the romance between Alice and Freda, including the unspoken topic about which everyone had been wondering. Callendar, Sim, and Turner boldly revealed that they had found no evidence of "sexual love" between Alice and Freda, even though the couple had spent nights together, and had been physically affectionate. But, the doctors hastened to add, Alice's feelings were indeed "unnatural," and that she had formed a "morbid perverted attachment" to Freda.

And yet, a "morbid perverted attachment" to Freda was not what the doctors ultimately deemed insane. Their attention was drawn to Alice's plan to marry and support Freda, "an impossible idea" that convinced doctors that she was clinically insane.[110]

Dr. B.F. Turner, the least tenured of these men, found Alice's desire to be economically self-sufficient—which, in this case, meant posing as a man—totally absurd, trumped only by her preposterous idea of same-sex marriage. He shared a part of their conversation, in which he pressed Alice about the impossibility of procreation between two women. A childless home, to his mind, served no purpose, and could only be understood as another sign of unreason.

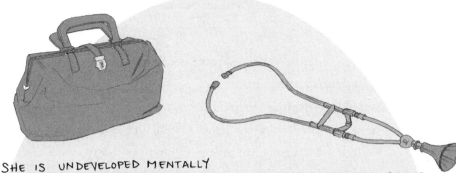

SHE IS UNDEVELOPED MENTALLY
HER CONVERSATION IS THAT OF A PERSON MUCH YOUNGER THAN SHE IS
THERE IS A LACK OF SYMMETRY IN THE FACIAL CONFORMATION
SHE IS OF A NERVOUS TEMPERAMENT
HER LOVE WAS SUCH AS THE PASSION A BEAST FEELS FOR ITS OFFSPRING
SHE IS THE VICTIM OF EROTOMANIA, A SUBDIVISION OF SIMPLE INSANITY
SHE IS LEFT-HANDED
SHE IS THE LAST CHILD BORN TO AN INSANE MOTHER
SHE WAS ECCENTRIC IN YOUTH
AT PUBERTY SHE DISPLAYED SYMPTOMS OF EXCITABILITY
SHE HAS ALWAYS FOUND BOYS MORE CONGENIAL AS PLAYMATES THAN GIRLS
SHE WAS THE VICTIM OF AN INSANE BUT AN IMPERATIVE DELUSION
SHE WAS VACILLATING
SHE BECAME MANIACAL
SHE IS OF LOW GRADE INTELLIGENCE
THERE IS A VACUITY IN HER CONVERSATION
SHE INTENDED TO COMMIT SUICIDE, BUT FORGOT
HER FACE IS LARGER ON ONE SIDE THAN THE OTHER
SHE IS TOO DANGEROUS TO BE TURNED LOOSE ON THE COMMUNITY
SHE IS VERY CHILDISH
SHE IS WEAK MINDED
SHE DOMINATED THE MIND OF FREDA WARD

"Alice, do you not know that you could not have married another young lady?" Dr. Turner had asked her.

"Oh, I could have married Freda," she replied.

"But some one usually has to support a family in a case like that."

"I know it, but I was going to work and support both," Alice explained.

"But a girl like you could not earn enough for both."

"But I was going to dress as a man . . ."

"But Miss Mitchell, do you not know that usually when young people get married they look forward to the time when they shall have children growing up around them?"

"Oh, yes sir."

"Well, did you and Freda propose to have children?"

"No, we were not going to have children."

"How do you know you were not?"

"Oh, I know we were not," Alice demurred.

Like Turner, Callender emphasized Alice's peculiar "logic" as a way to identify which of her desires were normal, and which were abnormal; it was, for the defense, a convenient mission of nineteenth-century psychiatry. Callender found Alice's plan to pass as a man and support Freda to be insane, concluding, "The frankness and sincerity of her manner on this topic was evidence either of a gross delusion or the conception of a person imbecile, or of a child without knowledge of the usual results of matrimony or the connubial state, or of the purpose of the organs of generation in the sexes."[111] The idea that Alice might imagine a life with Freda in childless terms was so foreign to the doctors that, in their estimation, it could only mean she lacked basic adult understanding of how sexual reproduction worked.

When it came to the act of murder, three out of the five experts believed Alice had been "dominated" by an insane desire to end Freda's life, displaying a total loss of self-control, another hallmark of turn-of-the-century psychiatric theory. On the stand, Turner used the analogy of a runaway horse, so strong the driver cannot control it.[112] Sale, however, believed Alice was suffering from "simple insanity," a version of "erotomania" that the defense had worked to avoid as a possible diagnosis. Interestingly, thirty-six-year-old Dr. Michael Campbell—who had almost agreed to testify on the state's behalf—declined to offer a diagnosis. He did, however, note that there were many patients in his asylum, the Eastern State Hospital for the Insane in nearby Knoxville, Tennessee, who appeared rational on most subjects.

All five, however, not only agreed that Alice was in some way insane, but also—and most conveniently for the Mitchells—incurable. At best, they warned, an asylum would offer her relief through "treatment."[113]

ATTORNEY GENERAL PETERS, lacking a single dissenting physician, nonetheless persevered. He pressed witnesses for limited definitions of same-sex love, and challenged them to substantiate claims that it was consistently emblematic of insanity. Campbell conceded it was not, though like Turner, he associated same-sex love with passions taken to an extreme. The always suggestive Sale testified that Alice and Freda's relationship illustrated the dangers of extreme passion, which he described as a pathological love.[114]

Unable to get much traction, Peters shifted his focus from love to marriage. Could two women marry? There was a known example, Peters pointed out. Annie Hindle, a male-impersonator who had performed at Broome's Variety Theater on Jefferson Street in Memphis, had been regarded as eccentric—but not insane—despite having married a woman. Turner rejected this line of questioning, explaining that two women could not experience "physical pleasure and giving birth to children." To his mind, these reasons alone precluded any ability to form a union.[115]

But could Alice and Freda have experienced "physical pleasure," the kind a man and woman enjoyed together?

The *Appeal Avalanche* wondered at Turners's point. After all, there had been no formal physical examination, and thus "it has not been proved that Alice could not perform the duties of a husband." Cases of indeterminate genitals, or hermaphrodites, were rarely introduced into polite conversation, let alone written about in newspapers consumed by the masses. Peters, however, would not request that Alice undergo a physical examination. Murderess or not, she was a respectable white woman from a prominent family, and her body was off limits—even if it played a large role in the case.[116]

"Was Freda Ward insane, too?" asked the prosecution. It was a rhetorical question. No, Campbell conceded, even though he had never met the deceased seventeen-year-old, and anyway, "she was dominated by Alice Mitchell, the stronger-willed of the two girls."[117]

"What about a man in her situation?" the prosecution further pressed. Has no man with sexual desires toward a woman ever committed murder? One need not be insane, possessed by perversion, to be driven to violence.

Sale granted that a man who committed a similar crime of passion "on the spur of the moment . . . is an ebullition that might occur in every normal man." But this case was not comparable, he maintained, and returned to the defense's central message, the argument that tied all of the testimony together: Alice thought she could marry Freda and work to support a childless union, that they could live like that indefinitely—an insane notion.[118]

After three days, the prosecution had failed to offer a convincing counterclaim, and inconsistencies did little to undermine the expert testimony. The Attorney General persevered, calling four witnesses who lacked expertise, but had actually known the deceased.

The state called Ada Volkmar, Freda's eldest sister, to testify first, but she offered the court very little new information, as did Christina Purnell, who

had witnessed the murder. The next witness, however, was not only new, but a highly anticipated arrival.

Freda's erstwhile beau and Alice's romantic rival, Ashley Roselle of Featherstone, Arkansas, took the stand, and the energy in the courtroom surged, with onlookers hoping for a plot twist. There was an outspoken group of spectators who shared William Volkmar's suspicion that a man was somehow involved. In this version of the story, Alice killed Freda not out of love for her, but to clear the way to marry Ashley.

Unfortunately for that camp, Ashley's testimony did little to support the theory. His courtship of Freda was largely unremarkable, though it bore her trademark theatrics. She wished to conceal the correspondence from her older sister, Ada, and thus used Alice as an intermediary. This arrangement continued until Alice read their letters and realized they were full of romantic sentiments, and increasingly serious in nature. After she refused to funnel any more of their letters, Freda broke it off with Ashley, but the explanation she offered was disingenuous. She lied and said that both Alice and Lillie had moved to Chicago, which meant that neither of her friends could serve as intermediaries any longer.

The state prodded Ashley to admit that Alice had expressed interest in him, but he denied it. There was no question, he testified, that Alice was exclusively fixated on Freda. During their conversations, she was interested in one thing and one thing only: getting Ashley to confirm or refute what Freda had told her about their relationship.

Ashley was in agreement with the prosecution on one front: Alice seemed perfectly sane. But just as soon as he had uttered those pivotal words, he cast a shadow of doubt on his assessment, recalling that, yes, she had spoken openly of a most violent act. But she did not threaten to harm Freda, or Ashley himself. The life she spoke of taking was her own.

By the time Ashley stepped down from the stand, the public was thoroughly disappointed. The next day, he was lambasted by the press. They took particular issue with the twenty-three-year-old postmaster's appearance, ridiculing his poorly formed mustache and "round, close cropped head, and his eyes [which] do not open very wide." His pink shirt, blue tie, and pants were mocked as ornate and unrefined. If any man was going to be able to tempt Alice Mitchell, the press agreed, it was not the foppish Ashley Roselle.[119]

CHAPTER SEVENTEEN

HER OWN BEST WITNESS

GANTT AND WRIGHT SPENT SIX MONTHS isolating Alice from the public, and the result had been near total control of the narrative. They were not about to let her testimony be the very thing that hanged her.

It was no surprise, then, that the moment Alice Mitchell was called to the stand, the defense jumped to their feet. They implored Judge DuBose to consider the upstanding Mitchell family of Memphis, who "may not care to have her made the object of scrutiny to some sensationalists." Indeed, Alice had arrived at the courthouse flanked by her male relations, but in comparison to Lillie, who was often described as meekly leaning on her father for support, the men of the Mitchell family appeared to be more shield than ballast.

Judge DuBose delayed the proceedings to check the legal precedent in his chambers, leaving Attorney General Peters irate. If Alice had convinced so many experts and good citizens of Memphis that she was insane, Peters taunted, her attorneys should be more than willing to let her demonstrate it on the stand.

While Peters grumbled and Judge DuBose deliberated, barely a murmur passed among the spectators. His draconian methods of courtroom control—unrelenting censure and ejection for relatively harmless infractions—now appeared to have a real purpose. The packed courtroom had waited so long for this very moment, on the most important day of the lunacy inquisition, that when it finally arrived, they remained perfectly still, spellbound by curiosity.

AT LONG LAST, IT WAS DECLARED: Alice Mitchell would testify.

Her short walk from the defense table to the witness stand was complicated by the swelling crowd. She had to maneuver past those seated and standing, who were quick to move aside. They were eager to make way for the star defendant, a woman who had captured the nation's attention, and yet, Alice had rarely been seen in public, and had hardly uttered a word aloud. After listening to people talk about her and Freda for the last six months, Alice's voice would finally be heard.

The courtroom watched with bated breath as Alice arranged herself on the chair, shifting and smoothing out her dress. They had become quite familiar with the back of her head during the lunacy inquisition, which is not to suggest that an obstructed view had ever stopped them from analyzing her; every diminutive gesture and expression had been subject to conjecture. Many had fixated on the way she calmly fanned herself during the long, oppressively humid days in court, judging her to be startlingly imperturbable. Others declared her furiously confident, content, and even cheerful. Of course, who could really claim such insight from their seat? They were barely able to make out her features during her quick entrances, and even speedier exits.

From underneath her wide-brimmed summer hat, Alice glanced over at the all-male, all-white jury, "selected from among the best citizens of Memphis," showing the rapt audience her profile. They gazed upon her in full view, and opinions were predictably varied. The room became a muffled cacophony of hushed tones and whispers as the crowd debated whether her oval face was pretty, or far too small for her body. Surely her features reflected her deviant acts, and spectators made sure to remember the shape of her nose.[120]

DuBose insisted on silence, and Peters launched into his line of questioning as soon as his voice could be heard. He wasted no time getting to the subject of Freda, although his opening question appeared relatively benign: How long, he asked, had they known each other?

"For as long as I remember," Alice said, her voice carrying to the back of the courtroom.

Of course, she had not known Freda her entire life. They had met at the Higbee School for Young Ladies, a fact she also denied. But her memory was not otherwise cloudy; she remembered every single date she saw Freda, and the many letters they exchanged.

Alice recalled visiting her ex-fiancé twice since her move to Golddust, once alone and on another occasion with Lillie. She offered small, insignificant details, like meeting a boarder in the Volkmar home during her first trip, along with far more consequential episodes, like her introduction to Ashley Roselle during the second visit. She denied having feelings for him, confirming Ashley's testimony; she had sought him out for the sole purpose of deducing his intentions with Freda.

"Did you know if he was in love with Miss Freda Ward?" Peters asked.

"Yes, I think he was," she answered, eyes watering.

Crimes of passion were rooted in jealousy, and Peters saw Alice's possessiveness and mistrust as integral to his argument. In his view, she was sane, and should be tried as a man would be in the same situation. "What made you think so?" the attorney general pressed.

"By the way Freda spoke of him and the letters I saw," she explained, handkerchief in hand.

Alice remembered this betrayal well. Freda had been afraid that her brother-in-law, the postmaster in Golddust, would notice that she was receiving letters, and tell his wife. Alice was happy to hold the letters for her beloved until the day she decided to open them, and learned Freda and Ashley were moving toward an engagement.

As tears streamed down her face, Alice told Peters of Freda's repeated flirtations, and explained how they drove her to extremes. She divulged details of the laudanum incident, and how she had tried to convince Freda to take it as well. She confirmed Lucy's account of another suicide attempt when she tried to turn the family's rifle on herself, but accidentally shot off a round in the process. And there was the incident before the murder, when Freda ignored her outside the photography gallery. The snub had so overwhelmed Alice that her shaking hands could not fetch the razor from her dress pocket in time.

"You intended to kill her?" Peters finally asked. The jury already knew much of what she had recounted, but premeditation was an important part of the prosecution's case.

"Yes."

"Why?" he quickly followed, hoping to finish the line of questioning before the defense could raise another objection.

"Because I could not have her."

At that, the *Commercial*, which had cast a shadow of doubt over the insanity plea from the beginning, was greatly affected by her testimony.

> The spectacle of a girl who has not yet reached her 20th
> birthday—one born of refined and [C]hristian parents, reared
> with the tenderest of care, amidst surroundings whose every
> influence was good—calmly and nonchalantly admitting the

perpetration of an awful crime, is rare enough and sad enough in all conscience. But that was not all. Into every horrid detail she entered with apparent relish.[121]

The paper's confusing portrayal of Alice—claiming that she was "nonchalant" about the crime but allegedly discussed it with "relish"—contradicts not just itself, but more importantly, the many reports of her crying on the stand. Had she flipped so wildly between emotions, from cool indifference to flagrant enjoyment, multiple sources surely would have noted it—with relish. Instead, a wealth of reporting indicates that Alice, still but a sheltered young woman, offered unflinchingly honest answers, to the best of her recollection, throughout the emotionally charged testimony. She had committed a terrible crime, to be sure, but she seemed far from the cold-blooded, self-satisfied villain depicted in the *Commercial*'s pages.

"Do you miss her now?" Peters continued.

"I have missed her every day since last summer," Alice said, her voice quivering. The season she named was not winter, when she had murdered Freda, but the previous summer, which she had hoped would represent the beginning of their life together as husband and wife in St. Louis. Instead, it had marked the start of their forced estrangement.

In stark contrast with earlier testimony from the Mitchell family, Alice made it perfectly clear that she did, in fact, understand that Freda was dead, and that she longed to see her beautiful face.

"Attractive?" he pressed, to which she answered yes.

Peters would have probably preferred to go further with this line of inquiry, but he would not have gotten far.

The *Commercial* praised DuBose for barring "revolting" details and "depraved, sensuous or degraded" interludes, and on this point, the *Appeal Avalanche* was in complete agreement.[122]

There has been a very close observance of proprieties and no disposition has been shown to harass the defendant, or to go to a line of investigation which, because of its suggestiveness, might have compromised her moral character.[123]

Peters yielded the floor to the defense, who approached Alice with caution. It had gone relatively well so far, and Wright was intent on keeping it that way. He played it safe, relying on topics that would remind the jury that Alice, at that very moment, was expressing the sentiments of an unsound mind. The obvious tact, then, was to ask his client open-ended questions about her plan to wed Freda, and what she imagined married life in St. Louis would be like.

Wright's approach worked on the *Appeal Avalanche,* who emphasized the marriage plot as the most salient indicator of her insanity. They compared the intention of one woman to marry another to "those of a child who would be capable of forming plans without taking into consideration the responsibilities of life."[124]

When Wright concluded—relieved, no doubt, if not optimistic about the public testimony his team had worked so hard to avoid—he was met with even better news: Peters declined further cross-examination. Alice's testimony had ended on just the right note for the defense. She made a quick exit from the witness stand, and began walking toward her father.

"Hold on, there! Come back!" Judge DuBose bellowed.

"Gentleman of the jury," he continued, once she had resumed her place on the stand, "do any of you wish to ask the defendant any questions, to examine her touching the condition of her mind?"

Major Fleece, one of the jurors, seized the opportunity, but he had heard enough about love and marriage. He was after macabre details, with a specific eye toward two of Alice's most distressing preoccupations.

"You say, Miss Mitchell, that you undertook to kill yourself?" he asked.

"Yes, sir."

"Do you feel regret that you failed?"

"I have always wanted to do it."

"Do you feel that you are determined to carry out that purpose?"

"No, sir. I don't know that I will," she answered, before concluding, "but I want to die."

"It was said you kept a thumbstall saturated with Freda's blood and yours," Fleece stated, addressing an oft invoked rumor. "Do you want to have that now? Would it give you pleasure to look upon it?"

"Yes, sir," she answered. "I think I would."

THERE WAS LITTLE TO ASK ALICE AFTER THAT. But as the papers noted, this was "the last act in the drama, and Judge DuBose wanted to savor it." He postponed deliberations until Saturday, July 30, so that he might prepare a written charge to read to the jury.[125]

When the day finally came, Judge DuBose delivered his statement, and then the jury filed out of the courtroom to deliberate—and returned within about twenty minutes.[126] The courtroom was so quiet, so full of anticipation that spectators in the very back of the courtroom, claiming the worst seats in the house, probably heard the wooden chairs creak as the jurors settled back into their seats.

The foreman, state senator Colonel McGalloway, was called upon to read the verdict.

"Presently Insane," he declared.

PART IV

CHAPTER EIGHTEEN

THAT STORY
WAS NEVER PRINTED

DECLARED INCURABLE BY LEADING medical experts and judged to be insane by a jury of the finest men in Memphis, Alice was remanded to the Western Hospital for the Insane in Bolivar, Tennessee.

She was to be committed on August 1, 1892. After six months of being a public figure—the subject of endless lurid speculation across the country—Alice was gone, out of sight in nearby Bolivar. The Wards silently accepted that justice would not be served, and returned home to Golddust. The big urban dailies called their reporters home, and the emptied city moved on.

WHEN ALICE ARRIVED IN BOLIVAR, the insane asylum was only in its third year of operation and already overcrowded. The third of its kind in Tennessee, the asylum was built to accommodate some 300 patients, divided by race and gender. But Alice's arrival pushed the asylum's population to 319, a number that would continue to rise. The luckiest among the

151 males and 168 females retained at least some semblance of privacy, but when patients began to number in the thousands, they were crowded into large dormitories.

Alice joined Bolivar's largest patient population, the 37 percent who had a "hereditary predisposition." This was followed closely by alcoholism and epilepsy in men, and for women, uterine trouble, those who suffered by the vaguely defined "ill health," and even the flu.

The only recorded therapy Alice received was "moral treatment." It should have entailed regular exercise, a healthy diet, some kind of work or hobbies to occupy the fragile mind, and occasional amusements, like dances, concerts, and magic lantern shows. Men farmed and went to workshops, while women did laundry and spent their days in the sewing room.[127]

But patients during this time period often received harsh treatment, and there was little oversight. The asylum staff was overworked, and they

were easily frustrated when patients receiving ineffectual treatment failed to progress.

Not that there was ever any expectation that Alice would "recover." The asylum was run and staffed by doctors who had declined the prosecution's requests to testify at the lunacy inquisition. There was no need to interview Alice, they had said, as the sensational news stories had already convinced them of her insanity. The year she was admitted, the asylum's own publication, the *Bolivar Bulletin,* reported that experts believed "her insanity is progressive, and it is only a question of time when this victim of erratic [sic] mania will be a driveling idiot through the decay of brain tissue."[128]

Of course, the efforts of George Mitchell could never be underestimated. He had, by that time, already proven to be highly effective at getting women in his family institutionalized. Alice had made the Mitchell family front page news, and it was easier to move on with her out of sight. Should the doctors ever consider releasing Alice, the Attorney General would have the option of reopening the case, but it seems unlikely George would have allowed that to happen.[129]

ALICE, WHETHER BY HER OWN VOLITION OR NOT, gave few interviews in the years that followed. When she did, the questions posed were curiously devoid of any reference to Freda, the murder, the inquisition, or her mental state. In a dubious article from March, 1893, Alice was described as a "bright, happy, laughing girl" who nonchalantly referred to the "tragedy that ruined her life."

These articles sought to reverse the public's conception of Alice as a perverted, masculine murderess. She now lived "in a pretty little room," which she kept neat before dashing off to spend her days doing the kinds of feminine activities she had allegedly shunned her entire life. At Bolivar,

she was said to love needlework, embroidery, and even reading—despite the fact that the Hypothetical Case had asserted she had shown "no taste for books or newspapers, and reads neither the one nor the other." She suddenly played the guitar, even though "efforts to teach her music and drawing were a failure" for the first nineteen years of her life.

The least believable claim of all: "The dances and concerts in the amusement hall were dull and spiritless without Alice Mitchell's presence. She dances well and never misses a set."[130]

Of course, if any of that were true, it would suggest that Alice was indeed on her way to "recovery," if not already capable of standing trial for murder—but that was not the goal of these articles. They assured the public that Alice was now tame and docile, and everyone was safe: she from herself, and from harming others. It comforted readers to see that Alice, at the end of the day, posed no serious threat to their values, or their class. She was now happy and feminine, vindicating their way of life. And if Alice was really the good, well-bred lady she was raised to be all along, the storm had passed.

Even the record itself hints that this public narrative of Alice was, as usual, not quite accurate. The *Bolivar Bulletin,* for example, concurred that Alice attended every dance, but did not specify whether or not they were mandatory. And their description of her refusal to dance with anyone other than male asylum attendants strongly suggests that the dances were indeed mandatory, and belies the image of her bringing jollity and high spirits to the amusement hall.

"No, I don't care to dance or have anything to do with Bolivar boys," she is reported to have said, "for I know they want to meet me merely for curiosity."[131]

ON THE LAST DAY OF MARCH, 1898, Alice Mitchell died. She was twenty-five years old.[132] There was no cause of death listed on the patient rolls, but the local papers declared her the victim of consumption. Alice appeared to be faring well, at least physically, until about 1897, when her health suddenly waned. She was described as "wasting away." Her body "gradually failed until the end came as it usually does to the insane—a collapse of the whole system."[133]

In Alice's case, consumption may have meant that she starved herself, which she had previously considered, or it could have meant tuberculosis, which was certainly on the rise at the asylum. Of the sixty-nine deaths from 1896 to 1898, twenty-three resulted from the respiratory disease referred to at the time as "phthisis pulmonalist."[134]

Alice's unexpected demise from tuberculosis could be easily reconciled with the account of her "happiness" at the asylum—but there is another possible explanation.

Thirty-two years after Alice died, Malcolm Rice Patterson made a startling admission. He told the *Commercial Appeal,* "Those closest to the case knew . . . she had taken her own life by jumping into a water tank on top of the building. But that story was never printed."[135] By his own description, Patterson would have been privy to this kind of information; he had represented Lillie Johnson in the trial, and had been employed by the same law firm that represented Alice, often supporting the defense's case and appearing alongside them in court.

Like much about her life, the story of Alice's death may have been a projection of the people around her, driven by fear and shaped by what they wanted to be true. We do not know exactly how Alice Mitchell died. We might never know. But we do know that it reunited her—almost—with her beloved: Alice and Freda were both buried at Elmwood Cemetery, about a quarter of a mile from each other. Because the Mitchells were of comfortable means, Alice was buried in a family plot, and her ornate headstone still stands; Freda's was unmarked until recently, when a tree was planted on the site.

ON HER WAY TO THE INSANE ASYLUM IN 1892, Alice made one last request.

During the inquisition, the Mitchell family had insisted that Alice, in her insanity, believed Freda was still alive, but if her own testimony on the stand had not convinced the public otherwise, her final stop should have:

Before being committed, Alice wanted to visit Freda's grave at Elmwood Cemetery.

Freda had no headstone, nor marker of any kind. Whether it had been a gesture of sympathy or much needed aid, Freda had been buried in a plot owned by the very same church she and Alice had hoped to be wed in. When Alice arrived at Elmwood on that August day, a year after they were forbidden to speak, she was trailed by reporters.

But even without a marker, Alice found Freda's plot, a mound of dirt that had settled while she was in jail. The spring had brought grass, and the summer wildflowers. At night, fireflies flew low, illuminating the ground.

What did Alice say to Freda? What was she thinking about? Was it the first time she saw Freda at Miss Higbee's? Did she imagine what their life would have been like, had they made it to St. Louis? Maybe she felt a jolt, like when a letter arrived from Freda, or when she picked the perfect rose for her beloved. Or maybe she thought about that photograph of her beautiful Freda, the one Alice had said she would not part with, even after they were forbidden to ever speak again.

But in the end, that photograph had been taken from her, along with the engagement ring she had engraved "From A. to F.," and all of the other treasures she kept hidden in her family's kitchen. It was all gone now.

We will never know what Alice was thinking at Elmwood that day, and neither did the journalists who watched from afar. But they did report what they saw, and, for once, what they wrote seems believable: Alice dropped to her knees and, for the woman she loved without shame, wept openly.

SEXUAL MONSTERS

THE MITCHELL-WARD CASE sparked a controversy in the medical community that would last for decades to come, as evidenced by a proliferation of articles in U.S. and European medical publications.

Dr. Frank Sim, an expert witness in Alice's lunacy inquisition, published the first lengthy account of the case on the *Memphis Medical Monthly*. His article was informed by sensational news stories and courtroom proceedings as much as medical research, and it circulated widely. It reached leading psychiatrist Richard von Krafft-Ebbing in Austria, who then cited it in the English translation of *Psychopathia Sexualis*, a forensic reference book for the law and medical communities.

By the time the 1894 edition was published, Krafft-Ebing had come to believe that "'forbidden friendships' flourish especially in penal institutions for females," but was on the rise more widely "partly owing to novels on the subject, and partly as a result of excessive work on sewing-machines, the sleeping of female servants in the same bed, seduction in schools by depraved pupils, or seduction of daughters by perverse servants."[136]

Alice, who met Freda at the Higbee School, fit into the third circumstance, "seduction in schools." Newspapers had initially speculated that Alice had been influenced by the first factor listed by Krafft-Ebing, specifically pointing to French novels about taboo relationships—but there is no evidence that Alice read these supposedly nefarious books, much less that the novels somehow led her to murder Freda.

The case provoked questions about treatment, sometimes leading to drastic conclusions. In light of Alice's murder trial, Dr. F.E. Daniel wondered if the medical community should "asexualize [i.e. castrate] all criminals of whatever class."[137] By 1893, Daniel had already deemed castration the solution to most cases of sexual deviancy, from bestiality to masturbation. He was a Southern eugenicist, a doctor who believed that the human population would be improved by discouraging reproduction among people with genetic defects, along with those who had inherited other undesirable traits. Daniel's call for castration of all classes was uncommon, but the school he subscribed to was not. Alice's same-sex love and insanity, supposedly inherited from her mother, could easily fall into these eugenicist categories. It was indeed the fact of her class—that she had been raised by a respectable family—that made Daniel consider *expanding* his categories to include such cases, rather than rethinking the categories themselves.

Voices of medical dissent, absent during the inquisitio itself, began to emerge afterward. Charles H. Hughes, M.D., president of the Barnes Medical College in St. Louis and editor of the *Alienist and Neurologist*, appeared to be the clearest voice of skepticism. He found Alice's plea of present insanity to be highly dubious, and in July of 1892, he began examining her case on the pages of his medical publication.[138] In an editorial, he criticized the sensational news coverage of the case, as well as the "novices in psychiatry" who would give credence to the insanity argument.[139] Nothing Hughes had read convinced him that Alice was insane at the time of the inquisition, or before it. Based on those articles, he understood the slaying of Freda Ward to be an act of revenge, and if Alice was indeed insane, "it will be because of other facts than that of contrary sexual feelings."[140]

Hughes soon moved on to the information newspapers purposefully avoided in their coverage. The same month that Alice committed to an insane asylum in Bolivar, he reprinted an editorial written by "H." in the *Medical Fortnightly*. It speculated that Alice likely discovered masturbation on her own, which she then introduced to Freda, and "mutual masturbation followed, then the well-developed perverted sexual love with all its disgusting details, was the almost inevitable result." The subsequent forced separation of Alice and Freda had made "sexual monsters of the two maidens—then the climax—murder."[141] Medical literature was still parsing the differences between hereditary and environmental influence—that is, whether the "insanity" was passed down from a parent, or whether the sexual relationship turned violent because of new circumstances.

Alice's case continued to complicate conceptions of class and female sexual deviancy. Prostitutes and promiscuous women—who were often poor—were considered sexual deviants, but their motivations were typically ascribed to economics, and the supposed lust and immorality prevalent among the vulgar masses. As Hughes and others who published on the case acknowledged, Alice made no economic gains from her relationship with Freda and, on the contrary, assumed a significant financial burden in her intention to pass as a man and support Alvin J. Ward's wife. Her desire to maintain middle class respectability seemed at odds with a sexually deviant woman, which is exactly why Alice's defense team had gone to such lengths to exaggerate her masculinity and attribute the murder to this supposed pathological crossing of gender norms. As Hughes was careful to point out, Alice, in her relationship with Freda, was in fact motivated by love, and wanted to enact conventional romantic feelings within the structure of a traditional marriage.

Nevertheless, others continued to champion the argument that Alice was insane, and that her insanity stemmed from her sexual preferences. James G. Kiernan, a leading sexologist in America, was a proponent of this theory. He had worked in asylums, taught in medical schools on the East Coast, contributed to leading journals, and was regularly called upon to offer expert testimony in the courtroom. In a lengthy article, Kiernan predicted "that sexual pervert crimes of all types are likely to increase, because of newspaper agitation on the subject, among hysterical females, from a desire to secure the notoriety dear to the hysteric heart."[142] Whether or not that came to pass, Kiernan was still asserting this view in 1916, when he identified Alice Mitchell as the reason American mothers had been keeping a watchful eye on female friendships, lest their daughters meet a similar fate as Freda.[143]

Kiernan argued that such maternal vigilance had proven successful, and there were fewer incidences of "sexual inversion" in America. Sexologists believed that sexual inverts experience an inborn reversal of gender traits, hence the emphasis on Alice's supposedly masculine inclinations.[144] Even so, interpretations of his research varied. Influential English sexologist Havelock Ellis studied Kiernan's conclusion and reached an opposing one, declaring that sexual inversion, or deviant "homosexuality," was actually on the rise in America. He referred to the Mitchell-Ward case to substantiate his claim in 1915.[145]

> The first conspicuous example of this tendency in recent times is the Memphis case (1892) in the United States....There is no reason to suppose that she was insane at the time of the murder. She was a typical invert of a very pronounced kind. Her mother had been insane and had homicidal impulses. She herself was considered unbalanced, and was masculine in her habits from her earliest years. Her face was obviously unsym-

metrical and she had an appearance of youthfulness below her age. She was not vicious, and had little knowledge of sexual matters, but when she kissed Freda she was ashamed of being seen, while Freda could see no reason for being ashamed . . . She was adjudicated insane.[146]

In the early twentieth century, middle to upper classes remained the focus of American research, but their proclivities were viewed in a variety of ways, rather than just the binary of "normal" and "deviant." In 1925, social reformer Katherine Bement Davis published *Factors in the Sex Life of Twenty-Two Hundred Women*, a groundbreaking study in the sexual activities of women, including auto-erotic practices and same-sex love. By the 1950s, Alfred Kinsey was conducting trailblazing research on homosexuality. The Kinsey scale indicated degrees of sexual orientation, from 0 (representing exclusively heterosexual) to 6 (for exclusively homosexual) because it "comes nearer to showing the many gradations that actually exist."[147]

But the rhetoric of deviance was far from extinct. In homes, the workplace, and academic and religious institutions throughout the United States, and most certainly in Memphis, the emphasis on marginalizing same-sex relationships persisted, echoed by politicians on issues of morality on a local and national level, and it became a powerful machine of degradation and political exclusion—much of which still exists today.[148]

LETTERS BETWEEN
ALICE MITCHELL AND FREDA WARD

FROM ALICE MITCHELL TO FREDA WARD

Memphis, Tenn., Sunday, May 11, 1891

"LOVE"—As I have nothing to do and nobody to talk to I will write to my Pitty Sing.[149] *Mattie has gone to church with Mr. Farl and Addie is talking to Frank and Ida. Will did not come today. I thought you might come this evening. I watched for you.*

Hun, please tell me why you thought that ivy would not grow; will you? I tell you almost anything you ask me.

FROM FREDA WARD TO ALICE MITCHELL

Golddust, Tenn., July 26, 18[91]

YBIR—Your letter was received and I enjoyed it, oh, so much, even if you did fuss at me all the way through it. Yes, loved one; I love Freda [Alice's alter ego] dearly, and I would give anything in this world (but A. J. W.) [Alvin J. Ward] if she had only lived. I wanted to see her so bad. We all [g]ot to talking about her this afternoon at Mrs. Matthews', and I couldn't help but cry. Mrs. M made them stop talking about [her]. She said she don't want to make me feel bad. I tried . . . not to cry, but I couldn't help it. I know you love me best. Love, I knew it long before Freda (YBIR) died. I know you are so sweet, but I love you better than any one in the world. Monday afternoon, Alvin, forgive me. I have done what you heard me tell Lil I was going to do. No, love, I am not keeping my promise, but I will be true to you this time and tell you all about it. Sweetheart, I didn't think what I was doing when I did it. I did not think I was deceiving you when I did it. But I more than worship you, sweetheart, and I only love A. R. [Ashley Roselle]. I swear I don't even love him now as much as I did when you were here. Believe me, Alvin, I am trying not to love him.

I didn't even think of doing such a thing until Lil told me to do it, and a week after you left this is what I wrote to him. Sweetheart, BELIEVE me, I will tell you the honest truth.

LETTERS FROM ALICE MITCHELL
AND LILLIE JOHNSON TO MEN

LETTER FROM ALICE (UNDER THE NAME "FREDA MITCHELL") AND LILLIE JOHNSON TO AN ACTOR THEY HAD MET ON THE ELECTRIC CAR LINE

Memphis, Tenn., Aug. 22, 1890

Mr. R. F. Chartrand:

KIND FRIEND—As you have been so kind to us, and you are going away, we thought we would return it by sending you a few flowers. Hoping this will not be the last time we see you, we remain yours truly,

FREDA MITCHELL and LILLIE JOHNSON

FROM ALICE MITCHELL (WRITING AS ANOTHER ONE OF HER ALTER EGOS, FREDA MYRNA WARD, AN ACTRESS)

Memphis, Tenn., Sept. 15, 1890

Unknown Friend—I am an actress. I have pearl-white teeth, blue eyes and light hair. I am 17 years of age, I have been in Memphis this summer with the Fishcer Opera Co. After I left Memphis I went to Greenville for three nights and then to St. Louis. I will not go on the stage this winter, and thought I would write you for a pastime, or what may follow. Next summer I will join the Fisher Opera Co. again, and next winter will travel with the "Said Pasha" Opera Company. I will not write to many, as I will be studying. I was going to join the Baker Opera Co. this winter, but I will rest and write to you. If I like you I will write to you while I am travelling, and tell you all that goes on. My home is in Memphis, but as I belong to a St. Louis troupe I am in St. Lois more than any other place.

Please send me your photo, and I will do the same. Well, I will not stop and write you a long letter next time. Hoping you will do the same, I am very truly yours.

Freda Ward

Please address Miss Freda Ward, care general delivery, Memphis, Tenn.

Memphis, Tenn. Sept. 17, 1890

My Own Dear Jim—Your appreciated letter was received yesterday with much pleasure. I knew very well Freda's Jim would not go back on her. He is too cute to do anything like that.

You may think I was joking, but, really, I admire you very much. I have written to others, and I think you are the nicest of the three. I prefer you and think I will drop the others entirely. I received a letter from one yesterday. I do not like him very much, and don't think I will answer it.

My dear Jim beats them all. He is my favorite.

I will wait once more for your photo, but this is the last time I will trust you. As you have kept your promises thus far, I suppose you will send it. It is to be hoped you will.

You are just the right age for me; you hit it exactly. I will always have you for my Jim, even if you do go back on me. I don't think I will ever forget you, dear Jim.

Yes, Freda Ward is my name. My true name is Freda Myra Ward, but my stage name is Myra Ward. I didn't change it much as most of them in the first troupe I joined didn't change their names at all.

I am glad you and your girl "don't speak as you pass by" or some other girl would be jealous. The fair commenced here yesterday. I expect I will go Wednesday.

I wish you were here to go with me. I would enjoy it so much if you were only with me. You asked me where my company plays when in St. Louis. Once when I was there, I played three nights at the Standard Theater, but the other times I played at the Grand Opera House. I have played everything from soub parts to tragedy roles. I do not care much for tragedy.

A comic opera suits me best. I dearly love the stage, and in fact, I enjoy my part. Little Lind has left the London Gaiety Company.

Ben Lodge, one of our troupe, wrote me week before last and said he was looking for a job. I heard from him Friday, and he is engaged as leading comedian of the Bancroft Opera Company. He is a great favorite in Boston, where the company appears.

As a professional, Miss Ruth Carpenter made her first appearance with Roland Reed in "The Woman Hater," as Alice Lane.

Will you please tell me the name of your chum that traveled with the company to which Edith Kingdon belonged?

I will not send you a lock of my hair this time, but as I admire you so much will be sure to send it next time, and it will be my own hair. Have you a photo of yourself that I could put in my watch? That is the latest here.

The little actress you were badly "gone on" last winter was Kate Castleton (or Mrs. Mary Phillips). I don't much blame you. She is cute. I am her height; not quite so flashy: my eyes are a darker blue, and my hair is the same color (although she wore a wig). I think she sings the "Spider and the Fly" and "I Dreamt I Dwelt in Marble Halls" in that play. It was "A Paper Doll."

I am almost certain it was the same one you were speaking of.

They have new words for the "Spider and the Fly" now.

I can truly say I have loved some boys, but I think if I would meet you I "wouldn't fall in love, but I would rise in love" with you.

I loved one of the actors last summer, and I think he thought a great deal of me, too, but he has joined the Said Pasha Opera company now. He will come back again this spring.

You come, too, and see if you can't get ahead of him. He is handsome, but I don't care for that.

There is one in St. Louis now that I love. He is not good looking, but I am almost certain he thinks more of me than I do of him. Don't get jealous, now, Jim. I don't intend to marry an actor: in fact, I think I am too young yet to.

Well, I think this letter long enough; longer than I expected.

Don't fall in love with another married actress before I come along.

Kate Castleton owns property in California. I suppose that is what you were after. Please write soon to your

Freda (Yes, I.L.Y.)[150]

FROM ALICE MITCHELL (WRITING AS ANOTHER ONE OF HER ALTER EGOS, FREDA WARD'S SISTER, WANDER) TO JIM IN WELLSVILLE, MO.

Memphis, Tenn., November 23, 1890

Dear Jim—I have heard Freda speak of you so much that I have come to the conclusion that I can love you also.

I am her sister and am the same size, same age, just like her and everything, except she is about an inch taller than I am, and she has dark blue eyes and I have dark brown.

She says your eyes are blue. I love blue eyes, although I prefer dark blue, but *of course you cannot get everything you wish for.*

Next Wednesday is my birthday. I will be 18.

You are just the right age for me, dear Jimmie. Have me for your sweetheart, will you, Jim dear?

I neither would want for my beau a silly little boy nor an old man. I think you will suit me exactly.

Darling Jim, please don't drop me as you did Freddie.

I had my photo taken last week, and every time the photographer looked at me I laughed.

In the end he took it while I was laughing.

Send me one of yours, and I will send you one of mine in return.

If you think Freddie is pretty you will think I am pretty, because you can hardly tell us apart, unless you look at our eyes.

I will not write any more this time, so write me a sweet letter Jim dear.

Yours truly,

Wander

Please address Miss Wander Ward, care of Edmonson's drug store, corner Lauderdale Street and Mississippi Avenue, Memphis, Tenn.

ALICE MITCHELL'S LAST LETTER AS FREDA WARD TO JIM IN WELLSVILLE, MO.

Memphis, Tenn., Nov. 20, 1890

Jim—If I have done or said anything to hurt your feelings please let me know. If not, please return my hair which I sent you, and oblige.

Freda Ward

LILLIE JOHNSON WRITING AS "JESSIE JAMES"
TO A MR. ROBINS (UNKNOWN RECIPIENT)

Memphis, Tenn., Nov. 30, 1890

Mr. Robins:

UNKNOWN FRIENDS—As I have heard Freda [Alice Mitchell's alter ego] speak of you so much, I thought I would write to you. Freda told me you were going to a candy pulling, and I hope you will enjoy yourself. I wish I was there to go with you. I know you will have a fine time. When you are pulling the candy just think of me.

I suppose you would like to have a description of myself as you have never heard of or seen me. I have light hair and blue eyes. I live in St. Louis, near Freda, on West Eighth Street near Charles Avenue. So you said you would exchange photos with Freda. I would like to do the same. Excuse this short letter as this is the first. I will write you a long one next time. Hoping to hear from you soon, I remain,

Yours truly,

JESSIE R. JAMES

P.S.—Please address Miss Jessie James, care general delivery, Memphis, Tenn. Write soon.

FROM ALICE MITCHELL (AS FREDA WARD) TO "VIRG" IN CARBON, TEXAS

Memphis, Tenn., Jan. 11, 1892

Dearest Virg—Your highly appreciated letter was enjoyed and read with much pleasure. I thought you had forgotten me. I waited until December 30 and you didn't come, so I then went to St. Louis with Jess [Lillie Johnson]. Had just an elegant time. Returned home night before last. Made a complete mash there. He just begged me to elope with him, but I loved some one better. A young man came to see Jess and me last evening and fell in love with my singing. I was real glad to be home with my friends again. Saw a great many pretty boys, but then their charms and sweet smiles are to me as naught when I think of one sweet boy in Texas. I would love to see you just splendid. I am quite fascinated with your letters, and also what is more previous your darling self. I am very sorry to hear of your illness and sincerely hope you will be able to come and see your Freda real soon. Certainly I will forgive you for not writing, as you were so ill. Give your brother my congratulations for me. I hope he has a sweet pretty girl. I hope you won't get married, dear, until you see me. I love you. I didn't realize what real love was until you stopped writing, and I looked for you all in vain. Dearest, I love you devotedly. I have one question to ask you, and you must be sure and answer. Would you associate with an actress? I won't worry you with a long letter, as you are not well. Please write a long letter real soon.

Yours, forever, FREDA

ARCHIVES

Memphis and Shelby County Room, Memphis Public Library. Memphis, Tennessee

Shelby County Archives. Memphis, Tennessee

Tennessee State Library and Archives. Nashville, Tennessee

CITY DIRECTORIES AND GOVERNMENT RECORDS

Memphis Board of Commissioners. *Report of Chief of Police*. Tennessee, 1892.

Dow's Memphis Directory. Tennessee, 1892.

R. L. Polk and Co.'s Memphis Directory. Tennessee, 1892.

Tennessee State Board of Charities. *Report to the General Assembly*. Tennessee, 1896.

Tennessee Western State Hospital for the Insane. *Biennial Reports*. Bolivar, Tennessee, 1890-92, 1892-94, 1896-98.

ILLUSTRATIONS

Pages 8, 9, 30: Memphis and Shelby County Room, Memphis Public Library. Memphis, Tennessee.

Pages 84, 87: Shelby Country Archives. Memphis, Tennessee.

PERIODICALS

Atchison Champion. Kansas, 1892.

Bolivar Bulletin. Tennessee, 1892-98.

Memphis Appeal Avalanche. Tennessee, 1892.

Memphis Commercial. Tennessee, 1892.

Memphis Commercial Appeal. Tennessee, 1898, 1930.

Memphis Evening Scimitar. Tennessee, 1892.

Memphis Medical Monthly. Tennessee, 1892.

Memphis Public Ledger. Tennessee, 1892.

Memphis Weekly Commercial. Tennessee, 1892.

Milwaukee Sentinel. Wisconsin, 1892.

New York Times. New York, 1892.

New York World. New York, 1892.

San Francisco Chronicle. California, 1892.

San Francisco Examiner. California, 1892.

San Francisco Morning Call. California, 1892.

PRIMARY SOURCES

Comstock, T.G. "Alice Mitchell of Memphis, A Case of Sexual Perversion or 'Urning' (A Paranoiac)." *New York Medical Times* 20 (1892-93): 170-73.

Daniel, F.E. "Castration of Sexual Perverts." *Texas Medical Journal* 9 (1893): 255-71.

Ellis, Havelock. *Sexual Inversion.* 1st American printing. Philadelphia: F.A. Davis, 1901.

Higbee School for Young Ladies. Annual Catalogs. Memphis and Shelby Country Room, Memphis Public Library.

Dr. H. "Gynomania." *The Medical Record* 19. no. 12 (Mar. 19, 1881).

Hughes, Charles H. "Alice Mitchell, the 'Sexual Pervert' and Her Crime." *Alienist and Neurologist* 13 (1892): 554-57.

_____. "Erotopathia—Morbid Erotism." *Alienist and Neurologist* 14 (1893): 531-78.

_____. "The Mitchell-Ward Tragedy." *Alienist and Neurologist* 13 (1892): 398-400.

Kiernan, James G. "Sexology: Increase of American Inversion." *Urologic and Cutaneous Review* 20 (1916): 44-49.

Krafft-Ebbing, Richard von. *Psychopathia Sexualis with Especial Reference to Contrary Sexual Instinct.* Translated from the twelfth and final edition by Brian King. Burbank, Calif.: Bloat Publishing, 1999.

Wells, Ida B. *Southern Horrors: Lynch Law and All Its Phases.* New York: New York Age, 1892.

_____. *Crusade for Justice: The Autobiography of Ida B. Wells.* Chicago: University of Chicago Press, 1991.

SECONDARY SOURCES

Anderson, Benedict. *Imagined Communities: Reflections on the Origin and Spread of Nationalism*. London: Verso, 1983.

Auerbach, Nina. *Private Theatricals: The Lives of the Victorians*. Cambridge: Harvard University Press, 1990.

Ayers, Edward. *The Promise of the New South: Life after Reconstruction—15th Anniversary Edition*. New York: Oxford University Press, 2007.

Bederman, Gail. *Manhood and Civilization: A Cultural History of Gender and Race in the United States, 1880-1917*. Chicago: University of Chicago Press, 1996.

Berkeley, Kathleen C. *"Like a Plague of Locusts": From Antebellum Town to a New South City, Memphis, Tennessee, 1850-1880*. New York: Garland Publishing, 1991.

The Black Public Sphere Collective, eds. *The Black Public Sphere: A Public Culture Book*. Chicago: University of Chicago Press, 1995.

Bland, Lucy, and Laura Doan, eds. *Sexology in Culture: Labeling Bodies and Desires*. Chicago: University of Chicago Press, 1999.

Bredbenner, Candice Lewis. *A Nationality of Her Own: Women, Marriage and the Law of Citizenship*. Berkeley: University of California Press, 1998.

Browne, Blaine T., and Robert C. Cottrell. *Lives and Times: Individuals and Issues in American History: Since 1865*. Lanham, Maryland: Rowman & Littlefield Publishers, 2009.

Butler, Judith. *Gender Trouble: Feminism and the Subversion of Identity*. New York: Routledge, 2006.

Coppock, Paul. *Memphis Memoirs*. Memphis: Memphis State University Press, 1980.

_____. *Memphis Sketches*. Memphis: Friends of Memphis and Shelby County Libraries, 1976.

Cohen, Ed. *Talk on the Wilde Side: Toward a Genealogy of a Discourse on Male Sexualities*. New York: Routledge, 1992.

D'Emilio, John, and Estelle Freedman. *Intimate Matters: A History of Sexuality in America*. Chicago: University of Chicago Press, 1988.

Diggs, Marylynne. "Romantic Friends or a 'Different Race of Creatures'? The Representation of Lesbian Pathology in Nineteenth-Century American." *Feminist Studies* 21, no. 2 (1995): 317-40.

Duggan, Lisa. *Sapphic Slashers: Sex, Violence, and American Modernity*. Durham: Duke University Press, 2001.

Edwards, Laura F. *Gendered Strife and Confusion*. Champaign: University of Illinois Press, 1997.

Evans, Sara. *Born for Liberty: A History of Women in America.* New York: The Free Press, 1997.

Foucault, Michel. *The History of Sexuality. Vol. I, An Introduction.* Trans. Robert Hurley. New York: Vintage, 1990.

Fradenburg, Louis O., and Carla Freccero. "Introduction: The Pleasures of History." *GLQ: A Journal of Gay and Lesbian Studies* 1, no. 4 (1995): 371-84.

Fraser, Walter J., Jr. "Three Views of Old Higbee School." *West Tennessee Historical Society Papers*, no. 20 (1996): 46-60.

Gilman, Sander L. *Difference and Pathology: Stereotypes of Sexuality, Race, and Madness.* Ithaca: Cornell University Press, 1985.

Harkins, John E. *Metropolis of the American Nile: An Illustrated History of Memphis and Shelby County.* Woodland Hills, Calif.: Windsor Publications, 1982.

Harris, Ruth. *Murder and Madness: Medicine, Law and Society and the Fin de Siecle.* Oxford: Oxford University Press, 1989.

Hodes, Martha. *White Women, Black Men: Illicit Sex in the Nineteenth-Century South.* New Haven: Yale University Press, 1997.

Hutchins, Fred L. *What Happened in Memphis.* Kingsport, Tenn.: Kingsport Press, 1965.

Jones, Ann. *Women Who Kill.* New York: The Feminist Press at CUNY, 2009.

Katz, Jonathan Ned. *Gay American History: Lesbians and Gay Men in the U.S.A.* New York: Plume, 1992.

Kennedy, Elizabeth Lapovsky, and Madeline D. Davis. *Boots of Leather, Slippers of Gold: The History of a Lesbian Community.* New York: Routledge, 1993.

Leavitt, Judith Walzer. *Women and Health in America: Historical Readings.* Wisconsin: University of Wisconsin Press, 1999.

Lindquist, Lisa J. "Images of Alice: Gender, Deviancy, and a Love Murder in Memphis." *Journal of the History of Sexuality* 6, no. 1 (winter 1995): 30-61.

Maeder, Thomas. *Crime and Madness: The Origins and Evolution of the Insanity Defense.* New York: Harper and Row, 1985.

McArthur, Benjamin. *Actors and American Culture, 1880-1920.* Philadelphia: Temple University Press, 1984.

McHugh, Kathleen Anne. *American Domesticity: From How-to Manual to Hollywood Melodrama.* New York: Oxford University Press, 1999.

Miller, William D. "Rural Ideals in Memphis at the Turn of the Century." *West Tennessee Historical Society Papers*, no. 4 (1950): 41-49.

Newman, Louise Michele, *White Women's Rights: The Racial Origins of Feminism in the United States*. New York: Oxford University Press, 1999.

Newton, Esther. "The Mythic Mannish Lesbian: Radclyffe Hall and the New Woman." In *Hidden from History: Reclaiming the Gay and Lesbian Past*. Edited by Martin Bauml Duberman, Martha Vicinus, and George Chauncey Jr. New York: New American Library, 1989.

Odem, Mary. *Delinquent Daughters: Protecting and Policing Adolescent Female Sexuality in the United States, 1885-1920*. Chapel Hill: University of North Carolina Press, 1995.

Phillips, Margaret I. *The Governors of Tennessee*. Gretna, Louisiana: Pelican, 1978.

Rosenberg, Charles. *The Trial of the Assassin Guiteau: Psychiatry and Law in the Gilded Age*. Chicago: University of Chicago Press, 1995.

Robbins, Bruce, ed. *The Phantom Public Sphere*. Minneapolis: University of Minnesota Press, 1993.

Schudson, Michael. *Discovering the News: A Social History of American Newspapers*. New York: Basic Books, 1981.

Sicherman, Barbara. *The Quest for Mental Health in America, 1880-1917*. New York: Arno Press, 1980.

Sigafoos, Robert A. *Cotton Row to Beale Street: A Business History of Memphis*. Memphis: Memphis State University Press, 1979.

Smith-Rosenberg, Carroll. *Disorderly Conduct: Visions of Gender in Victorian American*. New York: Oxford University Press, 1986.

Stone, R. French. *Biography of Eminent American Physicians and Surgeons*. Indianapolis: Carlon and Hollenbeck, 1894.

Terry, Jennifer. *An American Obsession: Science, Medicine, and Homosexuality in Modern Society*. Chicago: University of Chicago Press, 1999.

Taylor, Peter. *Modernities: A Geohistorical Interpretation*. Minneapolis: University of Minnesota Press, 1999.

Tolnay, Stewart E., and E. M. Beck. *A Festival of Violence: An Analysis of Southern Lynchings, 1882-1930*. Urbana: University of Illinois Press, 1995.

Tuke, Hack. A *Dictionary of Psychological Medicine*, 2 vols. Philadelphia: P. Blakiston's Son & Co., 1892.

Ullman, Sharon R. *Sex Seen: The Emergence of Modern Sexuality in America*. Berkeley: University of California Press, 1998.

Walker, Hugh. "A Crime of Passion? The Day the Doctor Shot the General." *The Nashville Tennessean Magazine*, July 14, 1963.

Walkowitz, Judith R., *City of Dreadful Delight: Narratives of Sexual Danger in Late Victorian London.* Chicago: University of Chicago Press, 1992.

Welter, Barbara. "The Cult of True Womanhood: 1820-1860." *American Quarterly* 18, no. 2, part 1 (Summer, 1966): 141-74.

Wrenn, Lynette Boney. *Crisis and Commission Government in Memphis: Elite Rule in a Gilded Age City.* Knoxville: University of Tennessee Press, 1998.

Young, J. P. *The Standard History of Memphis, Tennessee.* Knoxville: H.W. Crew & Co., 1912.

INTRODUCTION

[1] My research began with the following works, all of which pointed me in different directions. Their approaches influenced my own, whether I agreed or disagreed, and I'm grateful to Lisa J. Lindquist, who wrote the article "Images of Alice: Gender, Deviancy, and a Love Murder in Memphis," *Journal of History of Sexuality*, no. 1 (Winter, 1995): 30-61; Lillian Faderman briefly discussed the case in *Surpassing the Love of Men: Romantic Friendships and Love Between Women from the Renaissance to the Present* (New York: Harper Paperbacks, 1988); Lisa Duggan, *Sapphic Slashers: Sex, Violence, and American Modernity* (Durham: Duke University Press, 2001); Jonathan Ned Katz, *Gay American History* (New York: Plume, 1992)

CHAPTER 1: I DON'T CARE IF I'M HUNG!

[2] As I mentioned in the introduction, I looked for agreement among multiple newspaper articles, eyewitness accounts, and courtroom documents, and then chose to quote and add description where I found agreement or obvious disagreement with what was being quoted versus described. The same articles from 1892 (and a few from the years that followed), and the hypothetical case, were mined for information that was then distributed throughout the book.

[3] These events, and all that follow, have been reconstructed from newspaper articles and testimony.

CHAPTER 2: THE GREAT DRAMA

[4] Lillian Faderman, *Odd Girls and Twilight Lovers: A History of Lesbian Life in Twentieth-Century America* (New York: Columbia University Press, 1991).

[5] Of course, I am not suggesting that marriage would have fixed their issues. On the contrary, I point to their ongoing issues of jealousy and infidelity throughout the book. I am simply suggesting that the only narrative that Alice *might* have found solace in was one in which she and Freda made a home together, but I suspect the reality would have proven difficult, to say the least. Vincent Astor, the local historian I mention in the Introduction, said to me, "I fear what would have happened if they made it to St. Louis." I, too, have often wondered how these two sheltered young women would have fared out in the world, far from their families and unable to contact them. Would Freda's infidelity have disappeared, as promised, with marriage? Would Alice's jealousy subside, regardless of whether or not Freda's behavior changed? What would have happened if Alice failed to make a convincing Alvin J. Ward? How would they have supported themselves? What if Alvin disappointed Freda? Would she have called her family or sought help? Was Alice's violence inevitable? What if their families found them in St. Louis? These are just some of the questions that come to mind—and they enter my mind quite often.

[6] The Higbee School for Young Ladies. Annual Catalog. Memphis and Shelby County Room, Memphis Public Library.

[7] Barbara Welter, "The Cult of True Womanhood: 1820-1860." *American Quarterly* 18, no. 2, part 1, (Summer, 1966): pp. 141-74.

[8] Robert A. Sigafoos, *Cotton Row to Beale Street: A Business History of Memphis* (Memphis: Memphis State University Press, 1979), 78.

CHAPTER 3: MR. AND MRS. ALVIN J. WARD

[9] "Still in Doubt," *Memphis Commercial*, July 20, 1892.

[10] Small changes have been made to glaring errors in reprints of the letters throughout the book, but otherwise spelling errors and inconsistencies have been left in. The letters that appear throughout the book were quoted and reprinted in the articles "Still in Doubt," July 20, 1892, 1; "Silly Letters," July 21, 1892; "None But Freda," July 22, 1892; "Myra Is a Myth," July 23, 1892; *Memphis Commercial*, and "Letters in Demand," *Memphis Appeal Avalanche*, Feb. 16, 1892.

CHAPTER 5: I THOUGHT YOU WERE A LADY

[11] Cornelia Ward, Freda's mother, was also buried in an unmarked grave in Elmwood in 1882.

[12] Page 7 of Chapter 14: The Hypothetical Case.

CHAPTER 7: EROTOMANIA

13 For more on Gantt and Wright's role as community leaders after the yellow fever outbreaks, see J.P. Young, *The Standard History of Memphis, Tennessee* (Knoxville: H.W. Crew, 1912). For more on Alice's lawyers, see Paul Coppock's *Memphis Memoirs* (Memphis: Memphis State University Press, 1980). There was another lawyer at the defense table, Pat Winters, but he served only as an advisor and did not speak.

14 Isabella Mitchell's hospitalizations will be discussed at greater length in Chapter 14: The Hypothetical Case.

15 For more about Memphis's newspaper publishing industry, see Paul Coppock, *Memphis Sketches* (Memphis: Friends of Memphis and Shelby County Libraries, 1976). The *Commercial* and the *Appeal Avalanche* have merged and are still in circulation under the combined name *Commercial Appeal*.

16 My understanding of the role of print capitalism was influenced by Benedict Anderson, *Imagined Communities: Reflections on the Origin and Spread of Nationalism* (London: Verso, 1983); John D. Stevens, *Sensationalism and the New York Press* (New York: Columbia University, 1991); Michael Schudson, *Discovering the News: A Social History of American Newspapers* (New York: Basic Books, 1981); and Judith R. Walkowitz, *City of Dreadful Delight: Narratives of Sexual Danger in Late Victorian London* (Chicago: University of Chicago Press, 1992).

17 Paul Coppock, *Memphis Sketches* (Memphis: Friends of Memphis and Shelby County Libraries, 1976), 130-132. Circulation figures appeared on the newspapers in the *R.L. Polk & Co's Memphis Directory* (1892) and *Memphis Directory*, vol. 30 (1892).

18 There would be a Lizzie whose case would be a *cause célèbre* that same year, but it would be in August, when Lizzie Andrew Borden was tried for the murders of her father, Andrew Jackson Borden, and stepmother, Abby Durfee Gray Borden, in Fall River, Massachusetts. She would later be acquitted. For more on her trial, see Ann Jones, *Women Who Kill* (New York: The Feminist Press at CUNY, 2009)

19 If Freda had indeed been "almost beheaded," it is hard to imagine she would have been able to take off running while Jo attempted to distract Alice, even momentarily, by calling her a "dirty dog."

20 "A Very Unnatural Crime," *Memphis Public Ledger*, Jan. 26, 1892.

21 "Miss Alice Mitchell's Lunacy," *Memphis Appeal Avalanche*, Jan. 27, 1892, 5.

22 It is entirely possible that George Mitchell had influenced his neighbor's narrative.

23 "I Loved Her So!" *Memphis Public Ledger*, Jan. 26, 1892.

24 "Made Love Like a Man, Alice Mitchell's Unseemly Conduct with a Girl in Cincinnati," *Memphis Appeal Avalanche*, Feb. 22, 1892, 5.

[25] Artistic emphasis is added here, and did not appear in the historic printing.

[26] The unnamed physician's identity was revealed to be E. P. Sale, who would later testify in Alice's lunacy inquisition.

[27] Daniel Hack Tuke, ed. *A Dictionary of Psychological Medicine*, 2 vols. (Philadelphia: P. Blakiston's Son & Co., 1892), vol. 1, 460.

[28] Neil McKenna, *The Secret Life of Oscar Wilde* (New York: Basic Books, 2009).

[29] "Miss Alice Mitchell's Lunacy, Counsel Have Confidence That Erotomania Can Be Established, The Perverted Affection of One Girl For Another," *Memphis Appeal Avalanche*, Feb. 4, 1892, 4.

[30] "The Case in Court," *Memphis Public Ledger*, Jan. 29, 1892, 2.

[31] "A Most Shocking Crime," *New York Times*, Jan. 26, 1892, 1.

[32] "Evidence!" *Memphis Commercial*, Feb. 23, 1892, 1.

[33] "Two Girls in Jail," *Memphis Appeal Avalanche*, Jan. 27, 1892, 5.

CHAPTER 8: MAIDEN PURITY

[34] "Miss Johnston Under Arrest" *Milwaukee Sentinel*, Jan. 27, 1892.

[35] "After tragedy…Did Allie Intend to Mar Miss Ward's Beauty?" *Memphis Commercial*, Jan. 27, 1892, 1. "The Recent Horror," *Memphis Appeal Avalanche*, Jan. 28, 1892, 5. "Murder's Aftermath," *Memphis Public Ledger*, Jan. 28, 1892, 2. "Who Is This Jessie James?" *Memphis Appeal Avalanche*, Jan. 29, 1892.

[36] "Strange Story," *The Atchison Champion*. Jan. 29, 1892.

[37] There were 5,177 arrests in Memphis in 1892. As readers will no doubt suspect, poor citizens in Memphis were arrested far more often than those of more comfortable means. Disorderly conduct, drunkenness, and vagrancy accounted for 1,887 of those arrests, and from there, the numbers for small crimes like gambling and using profane language are minimal. Memphis would later be known as the "Murder Capital of the World," but in 1892 there were minimal arrests for violent crime. Only fifteen arrests were made for murder, but as Chapter 13 suggests, that number is clearly too low. Only 817 women were arrested in 1892, of whom 77 percent were African Americans. Memphis Board of Commissioners, "Report of the Chief of Police," (1892), 202-5.

[38] "Bernhardt Jailed," *Memphis Public Ledger*, Feb. 17, 1892, 2. "The Case in Court," *Memphis Public Ledger*, Jan. 29, 1892, 2. "The Grand Jury Has the Case," *Memphis Appeal Avalanche*, Jan. 30, 1892, 5. "Both Are Arraigned" *Memphis Commercial*, Feb. 2, 1892.

[39] "At Rest in Elmwood," *Memphis Appeal Avalanche*, Jan 29, 1892.

40 "Murder's Aftermath," *Memphis Public Ledger*, Jan. 28, 1892.

41 "At Rest in Elmwood, *Memphis Appeal Avalanche*, Jan. 29, 1892.

CHAPTER 9: DELICATE HANDS, HORRIBLE DEED

42 Alice's plea was supposed to be representative of her present mental state—not her mental state at the time of the murder. However, the murder was indication of "prior insane" conduct, as was the behavior Gantt and Wright compiled in "The Hypothetical Case," which is discussed at length in Chapter 14. The defense would also have to prove that Alice had a physical malformation or disease of some kind and show how it enervated her mental state. Hereditary insanity would be also be established.

43 "Both Are Arraigned," *Memphis Commercial*, Feb, 2, 1892.

44 "Will Be Disappointed, An Expectant Throng Will Gather at the Court House Today," *Memphis Commercial*, Feb. 17, 1892.

45 "Letters in Demand," *Memphis Appeal Avalanche*, Feb. 16, 1892. For more information on "femness," see Elizabeth Lapovsky Kennedy and Madeline D. Davis's *Boots of Leather, Slippers of Gold: The History of a Lesbian Community* (New York: Routledge, 1993).

46 "Two Girls in Jail," *Memphis Appeal Avalanche*, Jan. 27, 1892.

47 "I Loved Her So!" *Memphis Public Ledger*, Jan. 26, 1892.

48 "Alice Mitchell's Crime," *New York World*, Jan. 31, 1892. "The Recent Horror," *Memphis Appeal Avalanche*, Jan. 28, 1892.

49 Isabella Mitchell's husband, stepson, and children would testify at the lunacy inquisition. She was the only immediate family member who did not testify. Neither the defense nor the prosecution called her to the stand.

50 "Two Girls in Jail," *Memphis Appeal Avalanche*, Jan. 27, 1892, 5. "The Case in Court," *Memphis Public Ledger*, Jan. 29, 1892, 2.

51 "More Room for Judge DuBose," *Memphis Appeal Avalanche*, February 11, 1892, 4.

52 Lynette Boney Wrenn, *Crisis and Commission Government in Memphis: Elite Rule in a Gilded Age City* (Knoxville: University of Tennessee Press, 1998), 138-39.

53 Like Alice and Freda, Judge DuBose is also buried at Elmwood Cemetery in Memphis—in an unmarked grave.

54 "Will Be Disappointed, An Expectant Throng Will Gather at the Court House Today," *Memphis Commercial*, Feb. 17, 1892, 2. For more information on racial politics and manhood, see Laura F. Edwards, *Gendered Strife and Confusion: The Political Culture of Reconstruction* (Champaign: University of Illinois Press, 1997).

55   Case name: *United States v. Stanley; United States v. Ryan; United States v. Nichols; United States v. Singleton; Robinson et ux. v. Memphis & Charleston R.R. Co.* Racial discrimination in jury selection remains a major issue in America to this day.

56   "Will Be Disappointed, An Expectant Throng Will Gather at the Court House To-Day," *Memphis Commercial*, Feb. 17, 1892.

57   "The Mitchell Case," *Memphis Appeal Avalanche*, Jan. 28, 1892, 4.

58   Of course, Native Americans had been challenging this narrative since Christopher Columbus "discovered" America.

CHAPTER 10: ATTENDANCE EVEN GREATER THAN OPENING DAY

59   This scene has been reconstructed based on testimony, "The Hypothetical Case," and newspaper articles in which more than three corroborated phrases or scenes.

60   For more on women as spectators, see Ann Jones, *Women Who Kill* (New York, The Feminist Press at CUNY, 2009).

61   The first Civil Rights Act of 1875—also known as the Enforcement Act—was intended to guarantee African Americans equal treatment, but it was ruled unconstitutional by the Supreme Court in 1883. In the first half of the 20th Century, Jim Crow laws, increased lynching, and limited opportunities led to the Great Migration: Six million African Americans left the south for the Northeast, the Midwest, and the West—usually sticking to urban areas. For more information on this subject, see Edward Ayers, *The Promise of the New South: Life after Reconstruction* (New York: Oxford University Press, 2007).

62   I rely on theatrical terms, and my understanding of public spectatorship was informed by Oskar Negt and Alexander Klug, *Public Sphere and Experience: Toward an Analysis of the Bourgeois and Proletarian Public Sphere*, trans. Peter Labany, Jamie Owen Daniel, and Assenka Oksiloff (Minneapolis: University of Minnesota Press, 1993).

63   "Second Day!" *Memphis Public Ledger*, Feb. 24, 1892, 1.

64   "The Pity of It," *Memphis Appeal Avalanche*, Feb. 26, 1892, 4. "The Criminal Court Goes On," *Memphis Appeal Avalanche*, Feb. 27, 1892, 5.

CHAPTER 11: QUITE A FLIRT

65   "Miss Mitchell's Trial," *New York Times*, Feb, 22, 1892. The defense was not alone in their desire to see the letters. Though one would think that jokes about murder were inappropriate in the aftermath of a teenage girl's slaying, there were plenty of

jokes made on the pages of local papers about discovering Peters's mangled body in the basement of the Press Club, killed by frustrated reporters.

66   "A Crime of Passion? The Day the Doctor Shot the General," *The Nashville Tennessean Magazine*, July 14, 1963, 8-9.

67   He was born Hamilton Rice Patterson in 1861, but five years later, his name was changed to Malcom; he continued to be called "Ham." He was admitted to the bar in 1883, and would serve as attorney general for Shelby County from 1894 to 1900. He moved on to the United States House of Representatives in his father's former district (the tenth), from 1901 to 1906, before challenging his party's nomination for governor in 1906. He criticized his republican opponent, Henry Clay Evans, for supporting the Lodge Bill, which sought to protect the rights of black voters. During his tenure, he banned gambling on horse racing, enacted food and drug regulations, and signed the General Education Act (which established four colleges, including the University of Memphis), but his career ended in scandal. Edward W. Carmack, who had lost the nomination to Patterson in 1908, mocked Patterson's advisor, Colonel Duncan Cooper. Cooper and his son, Robin, ran into Carmack shortly thereafter on the street, and a shootout ensued. Robin was injured and Carmack died, but both Coopers (even though it was only Robin who engaged in the gunfight) were tried for murder. The public was enraged when Patterson pardoned his advisor; he had made 1,400 pardons during his time in office, and was accused of abusing his powers to aid his political allies. He later joined the Anti-Saloon League and supported Prohibition. By 1921, he was writing a column for the *Memphis Herald Courier*, and by 1923 he was appointed a judge in Shelby Court. A biographical sketch of his career can be found in the Malcom Rice Patterson Papers, Tennessee State Library and Archives. "Evidence!" *Memphis Commercial*, Feb. 23, 1892, 1.

68   Flirting on trains was an unenforceable concern for the men who sought to regulate it. In 1897, Representative Prichard B. Hoot introduced a bill to regulate flirting on trains in Missouri, but it was unsuccessful. That same year, Senator James G. McCune recommended Virginia make flirting a misdemeanor.

69   "Present Insanity," *Memphis Appeal Avalanche*, Feb. 2, 1892, 5.

70   "Unfolded," *Memphis Commercial*, Feb. 24, 1892, 1.

71   Ibid.

72   Ibid.

CHAPTER 12: FAIR LILLIE

73 "Fair Lillie," *Memphis Appeal Avalanche*, Feb. 25, 1892, 3. "Fair Lillie," *Memphis Commercial*, Feb. 25, 1892, 3.

74 Ibid.

75 "Second Day!" *Memphis Public Ledger*, Feb. 24, 189, 1.

76 "Fair Lillie," *Memphis Commercial*, Feb. 25, 1892, 1.

77 Lillie Is at Home," *Memphis Appeal Avalanche*, Feb. 28, 1892, 5.

78 "She Is Out on Bail," *Memphis Commercial*, Feb. 28. 1892.

CHAPTER 13: THE OLD THREAD-BARE LIE

79 "The Great Actress Wanted to See Miss Alice Mitchell," the *Memphis Appeal Avalanche* exclaimed, but even Sarah Bernhardt could not breach the defense's strict policy of denying access. The French actress, who was arguably the most famous of her time, had been performing in Memphis during the case. To learn of the crime, she needed only descend the theater steps, but she likely encountered news of the same-sex murder alongside reviews of her own performances in *La Tosca, Fedora,* or *Jeanne d'Arc*. She and Alice shared more than just space on those pages. In "the sensational" opera, *La Tosca*, Bernhard played "a love sick" Floria, a celebrated opera singer who commits murder, and then kills herself.

But Bernhardt's failed attempt to see Alice was no social call. The theatrical nature of the same-sex love murder appealed to her, and she had reportedly compiled clippings related to the case in a scrapbook. She wished to collaborate with French dramatist Victorien Sardou to turn the tragedy of Alice and Freda into an opera. The *Appeal Avalanche* made much ado of the rumored opera, imagining it "will not be wanting in thrilling situations and sensational development." The newspaper offered its own artistic interpretations of the theatrical show and, most importantly, speculated over which role the great Belle Époque actress should play. Editorialists thought Freda's part too brief, and Alice's too violent, but Lillie Johnson, the case's swooning, innocent darling, seemed like just the right role.

Nothing ever came of Bernhard's visit, but if Alice had actually been asked if she would like to receive the actress, she may have done so to honor Freda's memory. In happier times, the doomed couple had gone to the Grand Opera House and various theaters together—that is, the respectable ones with audiences free of mixed classes and races. They probably went unescorted, which had become increasingly acceptable at the time, offering Alice and Freda a tiny taste of freedom and independence. It gave each girl, in her own way, a means to imagine a world other than the one she knew. "Bernhard in the Jail....The Great Actress Wanted to See Alice Mitchell," *Memphis Appeal Avalanche*, Feb. 17, 1892.

80 Blaine T. Browne and Robert C. Cottrell, *Lives and Times: Individuals and Issues in American History: Since 1865* (Lanham, Maryland, Rowman & Littlefield Publishers, 2009).

81 Ida B. Wells, *Crusade for Justice: The Autobiography of Ida B. Wells* (Chicago: University of Chicago Press, 1991).

82 I found Stewart Emory Tolnay's *A Festival of Violence: An Analysis of Southern Lynchings, 1882-1930* (Urbana: University of Illinois Press, 1995) to be an excellent resource, as well as *Lynching and Spectacle: Witness Racial Violence in America, 1890-1940* (Chapel Hill: The University of North Carolina Press, 2011). For more on Wells, see Martha Hodes, *White Women, Black Men: Illicit Sex in the Nineteenth-Century South* (New Haven: Yale University Press, 1997).

83 Ida B. Wells, *Crusade for Justice: The Autobiography of Ida B. Wells*.

84 For a thorough examination of the concurrent, but racially segregated lives of Alice Mitchell and Ida B. Wells, see Lisa Duggan's *Sapphic Slashers*.

85 Ida B. Wells-Barnett, *Southern Horrors: Lynch Law in All Its Phases* (New York: The New York Age, 1892).

86 Attorney General Peters, the Wards, and the Volkmars wanted Alice tried for murder, but the hanging of a white woman was a very different story.

87 In *Sapphic Slashers*, an academic book, Duggan presents the Mitchell-Ward case alongside the simultaneous lynching narrative.

88 In *Sapphic Slashers*, historian Lisa Duggan thoroughly explores these points. In the 1890s, the United States was cementing its national identity, and it was predicated upon maintaining the white home on a national level. Same-sex love and African American men and women were cogent threats to the rigid hierarchy of race and gender, and the reactions on a local level from the judge, jail, sheriff, and newspapers speak to the national construction of American modernity. For more information on American modernity, see Peter Taylor, *Modernities: A Geohistorical Interpretation* (Minneapolis: University of Minnesota Press, 1999).

CHAPTER 14: THE HYPOTHETICAL CASE

89 F. L. Sim, "Alice Mitchell Adjudged Insane," *Memphis Medical Monthly* (August 1892).

90 The Hypothetical Case was inspired by the long reports that medical journals had been running for decades. Medical experts would receive these reports and study them in advance of a court case. They would then testify to the diagnoses offered.

If the prosecution had found any medical experts, they would have likely provided their own hypothetical case.

91 Charles Rosenberg, *The Trial of the Assassin Guiteau: Psychiatry and Law in the Gilded Age* (Chicago: University of Chicago, 1968).

92 "Not a Murder," *Memphis Commercial*, July 31, 1892, 4.

93 According to The Hypothetical Case, Dr. Comstock, and others who weighed in. As I suggest throughout the text, I do not presume this evidence can be taken as fact. Postpartum depression, which accounts for many of Isabella's symptoms, is by no means an uncontested diagnosis today. Some experts find it to be somatic, while others maintain it is a psychological disorder.

Charlotte Perkins Gilman's short story, "The Wallpaper," was published in January, 1892—the same month that Alice murdered Freda. The story speaks, however, to Alice's mother, Isabella. It is a first-person collection of journal entries written by Jane, who has been confined to the upstairs bedroom of a house rented by her husband John, a physician. Jane has just given birth, and John believes she needs the "rest cure" and locks her in the nursery. There is a gate at the top of the stairs, and John, who leaves for work every day, controls Jane's access to the rest of the house. The nursery's windows are barred; her confinement is much like being institutionalized. Jane has been diagnosed with "temporary nervous depression—a slight hysterical tendency," and her mental health devolves as her confinement goes on and she is deprived of stimulation—just like Isabella's supposed stages accelerated, from puerperal insanity to recovery, in the hospital.

94 Melancholia could have meant many things in 1892. Isabella might have seemed sad or depressed, but as a new mother, she may have just been tired. Carroll Smith-Rosenberg's *Disorderly Conduct: Visions of Gender in Victorian American* (New York: Oxford University Press, 1986).

95 "Sane or Insane?" *Memphis Commercial*, July 19, 1892, 1.

96 The Hypothetical Case states Isabella Mitchell gave birth seven times, but only four adult children were on record, and that same number are buried in the family plot at Elmwood. Only one deceased child (the first one) is mentioned.

97 Judith Walzer Leavitt, *Women and Health in America: Historical Readings* (Madison: University of Wisconsin Press, 1999).

CHAPTER 15: VICARIOUS MENSTRUATION

98 Thomas Maeder, *Crime and Madness: The Origins and Evolution of the Insanity Defense* (New York: Harper and Row, 1985), 114.

———

99 "Still in Doubt," *Memphis Commercial*, July 20, 1892, 1. "None but Freda," July 22, "Myra Is a Myth," July 23, *Memphis Commercial*, 1892.

100 Vicarious menstruation is bleeding from a surface other than the mucous membrane of the uterine cavity. It occurs around the time when "normal" menstruation should take place, hence the emphasis on the onset "around the time [Alice's] womanhood was established."

101 "Silly Letters," July 21, 1 and "Not Love at All," July 24, *Memphis Commercial*, 1892.

102 "None but Freda," *Memphis Commercial*, July 22, 1892, 1.

103 "An Analysis of Love," *Memphis Appeal Avalanche*, July 24, 1892.

104 Ruth Harris, "Melodrama, Hysteria and Feminine Crimes of Passion in the Fin-de-Siècle." *History Workshop 25* (Spring 1988).

105 "Alice Mitchell Laughs," *New York World*, July 20, 1892, 1.

106 "None but Freda," *Memphis Commercial*, July 22, 1892. "Is This Murdered Girl Insane," *New York World*, July 1892.

CHAPTER 16: AN IMPOSSIBLE IDEA

107 "Not Love at All," July 24, "More Evidence," July 26, and "They All Agree," July 27, *Memphis Commercial*, 1892. "An Analysis of Love," July 24, "Diagnosis of Insanity," July 26, "The Deed of a Maniac," July 27, *Memphis Appeal Avalanche*, 1892. F.L. Sim, "Alice Mitchell Adjudged Insane," *Memphis Medical Monthly* (August 1892), 377-429.

108 Dr. Callender was best known for testifying in the case of Charles Guiteau, who was on trial for the assassination of President Garfield in 1881.

109 "The Deed of a Manic," *Memphis Appeal Avalanche*, July 27, 1892. "More Evidence," *Memphis Commercial*, July 26, 1892.

110 F. L. Sim, "Alice Mitchell Adjudged Insane," *Memphis Medical Monthly* (August 1892).

111 Ibid.

112 See Janet Ann Tighe, "A Question of Responsibility: The Development of American Forensic Psychiatry, 1838-1930." (Ph.D. diss., University of Pennsylvania, 1983).

113 "The Deed of a Maniac," *Memphis Appeal Avalanche*, July 27, 1892.

114 Ibid.

115 "More Evidence," *Memphis Commercial*, July 26, 1892.

116 F. L. Sim, "Alice Mitchell Adjudged Insane."

117 Ibid.

[118] "The Deed of a Maniac," *Memphis Appeal Avalanche*, July 27, 1892.

[119] "Her Own Best Witness," *Memphis Appeal Avalanche*, July 28, 1892.

CHAPTER 17: HER OWN BEST WITNESS

[120] Their attention to her features was just another thing to speculate about, but they may have been influenced by pseudoscience, such as physiognomy or phrenology. Physiognomy was the practice of assessing a person's personality traits from his or her outward appearance. Phrenology was focused on the human skull; the brain was considered the organ of the mind, thus certain areas have localized and specific functions. In order to determine an individual's psychological attributes, the skull must be felt and observed.

[121] "Her Own Story," *Memphis Commercial*, July 28, 1892.

[122] "Now a Murder," *Memphis Commercial*, July 31, 1892.

[123] "The Mitchell Case," *Memphis Appeal Avalanche*, July 31, 1892.

[124] "Her Own Best Winess," *Memphis Appeal Avalanche*, July 28, 1892.

[125] "The Last of Alice Mitchell," *Memphis Appeal Avalanche*, July 31, 1892. "Not a Murder," *Memphis Commercial*, July 31, 1892, and "Alice Mitchell Is Crazy," *New York World*, July 31, 1892. "The Mitchell Case," *Memphis Appeal Avalanche*, July 31, 1892.

[126] Alice had been somewhat inconsistent with the defense, but had ultimately helped Gantt and Wright achieve their aim. Her testimony made her lack of interest in young men abundantly clear. It also made clear her overwhelming love for another woman, so great she had intended to live out the rest of her life in costume, just so they could be together. Dr. Sim, one of the medical experts, would later write that she returned to the defense table with "an expression of satisfaction," but given that her last moments on the stand were spent describing her longstanding desire to die and a blood-soaked thumbstall, that seems like a dubious observation. Alice's testimony had satisfied the jury. It was the jury who made it known that they were prepared to deliberate immediately. Dr. Sim wrote they returned within moments, but most newspapers time it at twenty minutes.

CHAPTER 18: THAT STORY WAS NEVER PRINTED

[127] Report of the Board of Trustees of the Western Hospital for the Insane, 1890/92, 1892/1894, 1896/98.

[128] "Alice Mitchell is Insane," *Bolivar Bulletin*, Aug. 5, 1892. Patients who had entered an asylum by way of homicide charge were rarely discharged. For more informa-

tion, see Thomas Mader, *Crime and Madness: The Origins and Evolution of the Insanity Defense* (New York: Harper and Row, 1985).

129 If Alice had wanted to set the record straight without her father's intervention, she had but a few years to do so. George Mitchell died in 1896, and was buried in the family plot at Elmwood Cemetery. Two years later Alice joined him, followed by Isabella in 1917. If Gantt and Wright's legal fees took a toll on the Mitchell family, their headstones did not indicate it as they were carved in the ornate fashion of the day, but by the time Addie and Mattie joined in the late 1940s, the Great Depression may have taken its toll. Their graves are plain, lacking the roses that adorn Alice's headstone. It is worth noting the elder Mitchell sisters appeared unmarried, perhaps a realization of the fear that their family's supposed matrilineal insanity would taint their own prospects.

130 Edward H. Tayor, "Alice Mitchell," as excerpted in the *Bolivar Bulletin*, March 10, 1893. Also, see the hypothetical case in the appendix.

131 Sherre Dryden, "That Strange Girl: The Alice Mitchell Murder Case," DARE I (July 29-July 5, 1988): 4.

132 The patient rolls were numbered, with the first being the healthiest. She appeared on the last roster in July of 1897, though she was back up to the middle roster in January of the following year. Tennessee State Library and Archives: Department of Mental Health Record Group no. 94, Series no. 7: Lists/Rolls of Employees, Inmates, Patients, Pupils and Veterans, box no. 3, folders 1-10.

133 "Alice Mitchell Dead," *Memphis Commercial Appeal*, Apr. 1, 1898.

134 1896/1898 Biennial Report of the Western State Insane Asylum.

135 Paul Coppock, "Memphis' Strangest Love Murder Had All-Girl Cast," *Memphis Commercial*, Sept. 7, 1930.

EPILOGUE: SEXUAL MONSTERS

136 These two quotes come from *Psychopathia Sexualis* p. 428, 430. The first edition, published in 1886, listed four "cerebral neuroses," including parethesia, which Krafft-Ebbing defined as "misdirected sexual desire." Under that heading, he placed fetishism, masochism, sadism, transsexualism, and homosexuality.

137 R. E. Daniel, "Castration of Sexual Perverts," *Texas Medical Journal* 9, no. 6 (Dec. 1893): 255-71, quoted from page 263.

138 R. French Stone. *Biography of Eminent American Physicians and Surgeons* (Indianapolis: Carlson and Hollenbeck, 1894), 234-237.

139 Hughes also made quite a few mistakes in his editorial. He misunderstood Alice's

plea as "not guilty" by reasons of insanity, when Gantt and Wright sought that she be declared unfit to stand trial. He also confused Krafft-Ebbing's definitions of sexual perversion with other sexologists' definitions, and continued to do so in subsequent articles on the case, introducing biblical and evolutional frameworks.

[140] Charles H. Hughes, "Alice Mitchell, the 'Sexual Pervert' and Her Crime," *Alienist and Neurologist* 13, no. 3 (July 1892): 554-57.

[141] Editorial by "H." from the *Medical Fortnightly*, excerpted in the *Alienist and Neurologist* 13, no. 2 (Apr. 1892). The article certainly left an impression on Hughes, who not only repurposed it, but was still wondering, a year later, how much "mutual masturbation" had occurred between Alice and Freda, and how much it influenced their relationship's violent end. See Charles H. Hughes, "Erotopathia—Morbid Eroticism," *Alienist and Neurologist* 14, no. 4 (October 1893), pg. 535.

[142] James G. Kiernan, "Sexology: Increase of American Inversion," *Urologic and Coetaneous Review* (1916).

[143] In the 1970s, Alice Mitchell's story was finally recast. After the 1969 Stonewall Rebellion, civil rights, women's liberation, and second wave feminism, the past was mined for lesbians, and Alice, who had so clearly informed modern conceptions of female same-sex love, became an important person within this history. She remained a murderer, but one who had been fundamentally misunderstood during her lifetime, and for almost a hundred years after. Jonathan Ned Katz included the case in his groundbreaking *Gay American History* in 1976, which finally cast a critical eye on the original newspaper articles and publications, including Dr. Frank Sim's own *Memphis Medical Monthly*. In Tennessee, Fred Harris's 1975 essay, "Lesbian Slaying Shocked 'Gay Nineties' Memphians" appeared in the collection *Gaiety...Reflecting Gay Life in the South*, and Sherre Dryden's "That Strange Girl: The Alice Mitchell Murder Case" was published in DARE in 1988, Nashville's lesbian and gay newspaper. That same year, "Alice and Fred," a play by Dan Ellentuck, ran in New York City's oldest theater, the Cherry Lane, though the playwright moved the tragedy from Memphis to Albany, and seemed to amplify her interest in baseball.

[144] Richard von Krafft-Ebbing described female inversion as "the masculine soul, heaving in the female bosom."

[145] Ellis was influenced by his wife, Edith Lees. When they married, he was a 32-year-old virgin, and she openly preferred women. Ellis recounted her case in *Sexual Inversion*, as well as five first-person narratives she found on his behalf. None of those accounts contained the same-sex love as violence plot favored by American newspapers, or even cases in asylums. Lees had not found these women on the pages of

newspapers or in articles written by doctors in asylums, but out in the world, and they were women the Ellis' were likely to socialize with; all of the women, like Alice Mitchell, enjoyed at least a middle class existence. Ellis's analysis, however, was a mix of naturalizing and negative, an attempt at carving out a space without threatening the traditional home or domestic roles within it. He reinforced the idea that there was some masculinity to be found in the female invert, which made her easier to identify than her feminine counterpart, but this was easier to maintain in theory than practice.

On the whole, they are women who are not very robust and well developed, physically or nervously, and who are not well adapted for child-bearing, but who still possess many excellent qualities, and they are always womanly. One may, perhaps, say that they are the pick of the women whom the average man would pass by. No doubt, this is often the reason why they are open to homosexual advances, but I do not think it is the sole reason. So far as they may be said to constitute a class, they seem to possess a genuine, though not precisely sexual, preference for women over men, and it is this coldness, rather than lack of charm, which often renders men rather indifferent to them.

[146] The 1915 edition of *Sexual Inversion* is included as volume I, part 4, of Havelock Ellis, *Studies in the Psychology of Sex* (New York: Random House, 1942). Quoted from pp 201-2.

[147] Alfred C. Kinsey et al, *Sexual Behavior in the Human Male*. Philadelphia: W.B. Saunders Co. (1948).

[148] Of course, I am not suggesting this is exclusively an American problem. The degradation and exclusion I refer to in the epilogue exists all over the world, including many countries that still deny the very existence of same-sex love. For example, in 2013, Russian President Vladimir Putin signed a broad anti-gay bill just months after police were given the right to arrest foreign nationals they suspected of being gay. It classifies "homosexual propaganda" as pornography, and warned that any parent who tells their child that same-sex love is acceptable is subject to arrest, and can be fined by the state.

APPENDIX

[149] As with the additional letters, only minor spelling errors have been corrected.

[150] ILY was one of their more obvious ciphers, meaning I love you. We do not know

how Jim responded, or whether or not the post office held the letter for Freda, as it was addressed to her. Did she, always delighted by attention and intrigue, find the impersonation flattering, entertaining, or worrying? We do not know the answer to that, either. But we do know that Alice penned another, much longer letter to Jim just two days later—and that she played a convincing Freda. She wrote with an ambivalence that encouraged Jim's affections while also introducing a rivalry. Among her various supposed liaisons, he was, of course, her "favorite," just as Alice was Freda's. The emphasis on "keeping promises," however, sounds very much like the voice of Alice herself, as did her insistence that Jim thought of her less than she thought of him.

INDEX

ACKNOWLEDGEMENTS

I CARRIED ALICE AND FREDA'S STORY AROUND with me for years, but I didn't find a good home for it until Nicole Cliffe and Mallory Ortberg launched *The Toast* and made me their history columnist. They gave me a space to write the kinds of stories I've always wanted to— including Alice and Freda's heartbreaking saga.

Before the essay was published, I described it to Daniel Harmon, an editor who understood my desire to tell the girls' story in a very specific way. I'm grateful to the entire Pulp/HMH team, including Hallie Warshaw, Jo Beaton, and Ann Edwards, and Adam Grano, who designed the gorgeous cover. Thanks to interior designer Dasha Trojanek, copyeditor Pam McElroy, and Southern publicist Rich Rennicks.

I have long admired the work of Sally Klann, the book's illustrator, and she greatly exceeded my expectations. Sally read early drafts and listened to me describe no less than a hundred ideas, all of which she perfectly translated into stunning, nuanced visuals. Historian Mary Klann, Sally's sister, was my first reader in grad school, and did not escape that fate on this book.

I'm generally lucky when it comes to smart friends who mistakenly offer to read early drafts. After putting in long hours with her authors, Emily Clement made herself available to me for small moments of panic and big picture edits. The wonderful Daniel Jacobson, also an editor, painstakingly reviewed every single line, and managed to do so with the same kindness he's shown me for a decade. No one understood what I wanted to accomplish here more than Avi Steinberg, and he made crucial cuts, organizational suggestions, and line edits.

I spent a few weeks scouring archives in Tennessee, fueled by biscuits and aided by local historians, curators, and specialists. I'm particularly grateful to Wayne Dowdy at the Memphis Public Library, who provided research support long after I left the state, and the excellent archivists at the Shelby County Register/Archives, including Frank Stewart. I was lucky enough to find a random link to Audrey May of the MPL and the Memphis Gay and Lesbian Community Center early on. She put me in touch with, among others, Vincent Astor, who generously shared his research and gave me a personal tour of Elmwood Cemetery, as well as the Memphis waterfront. Dr. John Harkins was kind enough to answer my rapid-fire local history questions, and share his own collection, which included a catalog from the Higbee School.

My mother, Anne Bank, provided me with the hermetic retreat I needed to finish the first draft of this book, and Amelia Ashton's Aunt Betty generously put me up while I was researching in Nashville.

Years of honors tutorials with Professor Francis Dutra at the University of California, Santa Barbara, made a historian out of me. The encouragement I received from the late Richard Helgerson, chair of the English Department, as well as Professors Enda Duffy and Mark Maslin, was particularly meaningful to me. A nod to the Honors College at UCSB as well, which rewarded performance with greater challenges, access, and support, and very much enabled me to become the person I am today. At Columbia, the late Lindy Hess left her mark on me. At Sarah Lawrence, thesis advisor Eileen Cheng taught me how to approach and manage large research projects. I was lucky enough to take classes from Matilde Zimmermann, who became my unofficial Don. Our car rides home were one of my favorite parts of grad school. Susan Rabbiner, the Assistant Director of exhibitions at the New York Public Library, was the best boss I've ever had—and by far the most stylish. Throughout my time at the NYPL, Susan consistently told me I should become a writer, and her praise and encouragement meant the world to me.

My brother, Justin Taines, is my biggest fan, and I'm grateful for his love and support. My husband, Michael Coe, has been telling me to become a writer since the age of nineteen, and was wildly supportive when I took his advice a decade later. This book took over his life, too, which he tolerated with patience and humor. I'm sorry that my grandparents, Max Scharnocha and Hal and Sue Taines, didn't live to see my first book published, but I'm so grateful that they always believed it would happen.

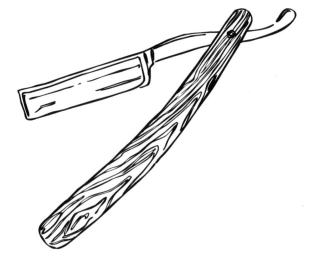